The Face Home-based Education 2:

Numbers, Support & Special Needs

CW00531687

by Mike Fortune-Wood

Part 2 of the results of research commissioned by
The *Centre for Personalised Education Trust*

Educational Heretics Press
in association with
'Personalised Education Now'

Published 2006 by Educational Heretics Press
113 Arundel Drive, Bramcote, Nottingham NG9 3FQ
Copyright © 2006 The Centre for Personalised Education
Trust

British Cataloguing in Publication Data

Fortune-Wood, Mike
      The Face of Home-based Education 2: Numbers,
      Support, Special Needs
      1. Home schooling – Great Britain 2. Home schooling
      – Research – Great Britain
      I Title
      371'.042'0941

ISBN-10:   1900219328

Cover design by John Haxby

Design and production: Educational Heretics Press

Printed by   Mastaprint Plus,
                 Sandiacre, Nottingham NG10 5AH

Contents

Introduction

Part 1: The Numbers Game

Chapter One: Pick a Number   1
    Questioning Local Education Authorities
    Results of the Freedom of Information Act Enquiry:
        i.   How many children overall are home educated
        ii. Growth in home education
        iii. The geographic distribution of home educated
            children
        iv. Home education by age and sex
        v.   De-registrations
        vi. School Attendance Orders and Educational
            Supervision Orders
        vii. Children with statements of special
            educational needs
        viii. Geographical distribution of home educated
            children with a statement
    Home Educators as a Lobby

Part 2: Support or Obstruction?

Chapter Two: Service Provision for Home Educators   15
    Diverse Support Structures
    The Quality of Support
        i.   Local contacts
        ii. Newsletters
        iii. Legal advice
        iv. Locating a lawyer
        v.   Home education in action
        vi. Sourcing free or cheap resources
        vii. Sourcing commercial learning resources
        viii. Obtaining discounts
        ix. Help in networking with other home
            educators
        x.   Exam information
        xi. Helping children to network and find
            contacts
        xii. Assistance in liaising with an LEA
        xiii. Informal social support
        xiv. Legislation and updates on current issues
        xv. Curriculum materials
        xvi. Support in dealing with statutory agencies
    Extrapolating Average Ratings on Quality of Service

Crucial Resources
Support at the Beginning of Home Educating
Support from Local Education Authorities
Drafting Letters
Ongoing and General Support
Diversity
Attitudes Towards State Involvement in Home Education
The Quality of Information Provided by LEAs:
    i. Home visits
    ii. Broad and balanced
    iii. Ongoing monitoring
    iv. De-registration
    v. Statements of Special Educational Need

Chapter Three: View from Local Education Authorities   39
An Agenda Gap?
DfES Draft Consultation Document for Guidance to LEAs in
England 2005
The LEA Responses
    i.   Child protection
    ii.   De-registrations
    iii. Compulsory Registration of Home Educators
    iv. Educational Assessment
    v.   SEN Statements
    vi. Reviewing Internal LEA Policies
    vii. Flexi-schooling
    viii. Costs
Conclusions

Chapter Four: But What About University?   57
From Prejudice to Misunderstanding
Finding Flexibility in University Admissions
The Open University: providing alternative pathways
Conclusions

Part 3: Special Educational Needs

Chapter 5: The Experience of Home Education in
       Families with Children with SENs   72
Reasons for Home Educating
The Implications of Home Educating a Child with Special
Needs
Relationships and SENs
Support Organisations and Children with SENs
LEAs and Children with SENs
Other Forms of Support for SEN

References   95

Acknowledgements:

This book represents the second phase of a research project into home education in the UK under the auspices of the charity the *Centre for Personalised Education Trust*. I am particularly indebted to the charity's trustees for their support and for making this research a priority. In particular Peter Humphries, Roland and Janet Meighan and John White from PEN have all played invaluable roles.

The fund-raising for the project has relied on three main sources; Roland and Janet Meighan have contributed generously from *Educational Heretics Press*, as have many individual members of PEN and Jan Fortune-Wood has worked hard to secure grant funding. We are particularly grateful to the *Esmée Fairbairn Trust* for their financial support.

Thanks to Stella Howden with her assistance formulating the questionnaire on special educational needs. Thanks to Clare Murton for her painstaking work researching the online policy statements of local education authorities and thanks to Jan Fortune-Wood for her assistance with the research and for extensively editing this text.

Most of all, thanks to all the home educating families who have taken the time to contribute to the research. One of our major aims is to develop a body of research which will assist home educators now and into the future, so thank you.

Mike Fortune-Wood
May 2006

Introduction

This book is the second in a series of publications following the life of an extensive programme of research into home-based education. In the first phase we considered questions of demographics, choice and methodology – who home educates, why do they do so and what kind of educational philosophy informs the provision of education at home. In this phase we have moved up a gear to consider the golden question of how many home educators there might currently be. This has always been a vexed issue. With no compunction to register with local education authorities, and good reasons for many home educators not to contact LEAs, previous attempts to estimate numbers have always run aground. In this research, I decided to take an innovative approach to the numbers research, using evidence from a series of enquiries to LEAs made possible by the Freedom of Information Act, and combining this with evidence from the home education community to arrive at a multiplier which gives the most accurate estimate to date.

This phase of the research is not concerned only with quantitative evidence. An area that has been neglected by much previous research is the arena of how home educators obtain support or access services. This will be an ongoing theme developed further in later research, but here I examine three key aspects of support networks, both voluntary and statutory, and how they serve or fail to serve the needs of home educators.

The focus is firstly on voluntary organisations; how is support provided and accessed and how is it perceived by those using it. Secondly, I look at the continuing problems that home educators routinely encounter in dealing with statutory authorities that persist in acting beyond the remit of their legal duties. This will be a theme that is expanded on in later research, but at this stage I again made use of the Freedom of Information Act to garner undiluted opinions of how a large sample of LEAs view home education. The results highlight a gap between the broad cultures of home education and the perceptions of those cultures by professionals.

A chapter from Jan Fortune-Wood extends the theme of support for, or obstruction of, home education with a consideration of how university admissions officers respond to home educators across a sample range of arts and science disciplines. With home education growing in popularity and more children reaching the end of their compulsory education years as home educators the question of how children move on from home education is becoming an increasingly pressing one. Later research will return to this theme to look at a broader range of options taken up by home educated young adults, but here the focus is on university entrance.

Finally, a group continually overlooked in research are given detailed attention. Home educators with special needs children face distinctive challenges in providing a suitable education, challenges which can be significantly eased or added to by both the home education community and a range of statutory agencies. Why do parents choose home education for their special needs children? What are the effects on parents of taking on this particular type of education at home? How are home educating families of special needs children supported or failed by informal and voluntary networks and professionals?

The research covered in this book provides strong indications for the future direction of research into home education. The gap between the needs of home educators and service provision, the problems of communicating a range of alternative educational philosophies to professionals who may turn out to have an agenda only tangentially focused on education, the lack of coherent thinking on how to include home educated children with non-standard educational backgrounds in higher education provision, and the risk of social exclusion for children with special needs are all matters that point to the need for more research across a range of participant, academic and professional boundaries.

Part one

The Numbers Game

Whenever a reporter contacts me to discuss home education the question of how many home educators there are in the country inevitably arises. The answer, however, is complicated and estimates have remained various. In this part of the research I used an enquiry under The Freedom of Information Act (FOI) to find a base-line figure of the number of home educators known to their local education authorities (LEAs). My principal aim in contacting LEAs, was to improve the accuracy of the estimates of how many home educators there are in the UK, but this enquiry could only ever provide part of the answer. Home educators do not need to register with their LEAs, and as far as we are aware, the government do not collect data or devise estimates on this subject. Paula Rothermel uses government data to estimate that their could be as many as 560,000 children of compulsory educational age in the UK not attending schools (Fortune-Wood, 2005, p.1). Rothermel, however, points out that the figure is tentative because much of the government data is itself estimated and, in any case, it is extremely improbable that all of these apparently 'missing' children are all home educated, but it does beg the question as to where are they.

Given that the national census office itself does not know exactly how many children there are in the country at any one time, estimates are bound to remain somewhat tentative. Government figures show that there were 8.32 million children of compulsory school age at the start of the 2003-2004 school year, these being the most up to date figures available. (DfES 2004) Of these 7.33 million (88%) attended maintained schools and 989.7 thousand (12%) attended non-maintained schools. These figures do not take account of home education as the government have no figures for how many home educated children there are. Due to the inherent problems of pinning down an accurate number, previous estimates of total numbers vary widely between 30,000 and 140,000 children.

Chapter One

Pick a Number

Finding out how many home educators there are has become an increasingly complex question. Not only are national statistics open to question and interpretation, and not only is there rightly no compulsion on home educators to register themselves with either local education authorities or the DfES, but there are also a number of other issues that can obscure the figure reached.

One such issue which arises in estimating numbers of home educators is the vexed question of how many home educators are 'genuine'. During meetings between myself and a number of LEA representatives over the last two years, a recurring claim of LEA officers is that they consider that some (perhaps even many) parents deregister their children from schools claiming to home educate, but with no intention or inclination to actually do so. The LEA position is that there is a persistent stream of parents who use de-registration from school as a strategy to avoid prosecution for truancy or to short circuit exclusions or some other school related problem. The effect of this claim is that these parents inflate the figures of 'true' home educators.

Such thinking is not only highly convoluted, but also problematic. Since these families are known to their LEAs, who have the power and even the duty to act if they have a genuine reason to believe that a family has no intention to home educate, the only reasonable conclusion is that in fact the LEA has insufficient grounds for issuing a school attendance order (SAO). It is not supportable that whole swathes of home educators can be discounted merely on the gut feelings of officers who are attempting to second guess which parents stated intention to home educate is 'real' or not. If parents say they are home educating and are not doing so then the law provides a mechanism to correct this. It was therefore, decided not to adjust the figures to account for this alleged group. In fact my previous research (Fortune-Wood, 2005, pp. 28-34) shows that a great many home educators begin to home educate precisely because they are experiencing a range of problems with schools, including school refusal and/or truancy issues, and that these families go on to successfully home educate their children regardless of the range of socio-economic backgrounds and educational histories of the families. It would not be correct, therefore, to exclude a percentage of families known to their LEAs from the figures for home educators.

Although the primary aim in contacting LEAs was to reach a base-line figure of home educators, it was decided to use the opportunity of making a FOI enquiry to ask a number of subsidiary questions. The purpose of these was to gain a better understanding of the relationship between LEAs and the home educating community. In particular, it was interesting to see the numbers of SAOs issued, the proportion of children being home educated and known to their LEAs who also have statements of special educational needs, the numbers of children de-registered in the previous twelve months, and how many families, as against how many children, were home educating.

Questioning Local Education Authorities

Since it was anticipated that some LEAs might take the view that the research project was not one that they wanted to allocate resources to or co-operate with I therefore decided that it was essential to make use of the Freedom of Information Act 2000. Since I had an existing database of LEAs in England and Wales I decided to restrict the research to those parts of the UK.

Eight questions were asked, some of which broke down into several parts. The first four questions concentrated on the over-riding numbers question. Question 1 asked for the total number of children an LEA was aware of as living in the area and of school age. This figure was further requested to be broken down by sex and into the age groups 5-11, 12-14 and 15-16 years old. Question 2 asked for a similar breakdown, but specifically in respect of home educated children of whom they were aware. Question 3 asked how many families were they aware of who were home educating their children and question 4 asked how many children had been deregistered in the last 12 months for which they had records. The reasons for choosing these particular age groups was to examine what proportions of primary school children, secondary school children not yet taking final examinations and secondary school children of the age for taking GCSE examinations were home educating as distinct categories.

Moving on to slightly broader issues, question 5 asked how many children in each LEA were statemented as having special needs whilst question 6 asked how many children being home educated currently held a statement of special needs. Finally, question 7 asked how many 'school attendance orders' each LEA had issued in the last 12 months and question 8 asked how many 'educational supervision orders' each LEA had issued in the last 12 months. The results were tabulated so as to allow me to analyse the results for the country as a whole as well as for each responding LEA.

Results of the Freedom of Information Act Enquiry

While most LEAs responded positively, on time and in a professional manner others either failed to respond at all or did so with unintelligible or clearly inaccurate data. It was clear from some of the replies that the understanding of the Freedom of Information Act was often sketchy. Following requests for clarification or correction and, in some cases a demand for a reply backed up by the Commissioner for Information, one hundred and nine LEAs responded.

i. How many children overall are home educated?

Overall the one hundred and nine LEAs that responded represented approximately 5 million children of compulsory educational age, more than half of all such children in the UK. There are approximately 8.3 million children of compulsory education age in the UK (DfES, 2006) However, it should be noted that the total number of children of compulsory school age varies considerably over the year, depending upon when the question is asked. If the question is raised in June then all children who are aged 5 through 16 inclusive are of compulsory school age, but in August then children who are have just had a fifth birthday will not yet be of compulsory school age, whilst those aged 16 will have already left school, so only some five-year-olds and those aged 6 through 15 inclusive are of compulsory educational age, reducing the numbers considerably. It is, therefore, impossible to arrive at a single accurate figure.

The responding LEAs knew of 10,862 children being home educated. We also knew the total number of children within the responding LEAs as well as the nearest estimate of the total number of children in the UK. This enabled me to work out what proportion of children living in the respondent LEAs and gave a ratio by which to multiply the figure of 10,862 children in order to determine the total number of children known to their LEAs and being home educated in the UK as a whole. This suggests that all LEAs and school boards are aware of over 18,100 home educated children. Since not all home educators are known to their LEAs, to complete the calculation and work out how many children are being home educated overall, it was also necessary needed to work out what proportion of home educated children are known by the LEA.

At the first large scale national conference of home educators in the UK in 2000 Malcolm Muckle (an innovative campaigner for home education rights) asked the gathering how many were known by their LEA. The results showed that significantly less than half of those attending were known by their LEA. This exercise has been repeated at a number of national gatherings since and has yielded similar results on every occasion. To confirm these proportions a number of people were contacted who are involved in organising local groups throughout the UK and asked a similar question. Group organisers consistently replied that between a third and half of their members indicated that they are known by their LEA. This proportion appears to have remained surprisingly stable over time and location.

It seems from this, therefore, that a reasonable way of estimating the total number home educators would be to multiply the number of known home educators by between 2 and 3 times. This yields a figure of 36,200 to 54,300 children or 45,250 children plus or minus 10 thousand. In short, approximately one half of one percent of all children of compulsory school age in the UK are being home educated or, put another way, 55 in every 10,000 children.

It should also be noted that since many children are removed from school and then returned to school at a later date the total number of children who experience home education at some time in their life will be far greater than this number.

ii. Growth in home education.

Since it is difficult to know how many children are home educated today it is even more difficult to know by how much it has grown. There are however some indications of dramatic growth in the popularity of home education in the UK.

The earliest attempt to identify how many home educators there were in the UK was conducted by Roland Meighan. In 1977 Meighan identified just 20 home educating families in the whole of the UK. In 1999 as part of a feasibility study Alan Thomas asked a number of local education authorities how many home educators they were aware of. The reply he received, when extrapolated to the whole of the country, suggested that LEAs were aware of around 6,000 children being home educated in England. This would in turn extrapolate to their being a little over 7,000 in the UK as a whole. However, as Thomas only approached 5 London based LEAs he rightly identifies this as an extremely tentative figure carrying with it many assumptions. If Thomas' results are treated in the same way as mine, to include a multiplier in order to take account of those home educators not known to LEAs then the figure of 7,000 'known' home educators becomes a total of between 14,000 and 21,000 in 1999. (See graph below).

Thus between 1999 and 2005 there was a growth of around two and a half times yielding an annual compound growth rate of approximately 17%. Taking Meighan's figure of just 20 home educated children in 1977 then the annual compound growth between 1977 and 1999 was 23.25 % albeit starting from a very low base figure.

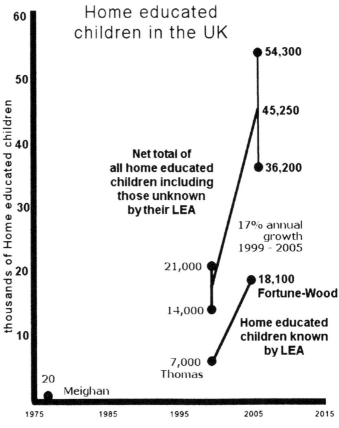

iii. The geographic distribution of home educated children

It seems from the survey that there is a wide variation of take up of the option to home educate. The greatest number of home educators in the study was in Kent where the LEA reported that they knew of 666 home educated children (yielding a possible total of between 1,300 to 2,000 children in this particular area, including those not known to the LEA). The LEA in the survey with the largest proportion of home educating children was Ceredigion with 1.1% (35 children being home educated). The Isle of Wight had the second largest proportion of home educated children with 52 children representing 0.6% of all children in the area being home educated. Both of these areas are rural with relatively few children living in the area. There is also anecdotal evidence that home educators move into these particular areas; to Ceredigion in search of a less stressful lifestyle and to the Isle of Wight because there is a well known and established local home education support group operating there.

iv. Home education by age and sex

Numbers of children known by LEAs to be home educated as a percentage of all children in the UK by age and sex:

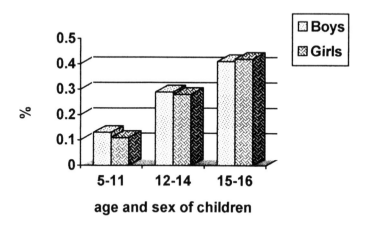

	Boys	Girls
5-11	0.13%	0.11%
12-14	0.29%	0.28%
15-16	0.41%	0.42%

There is remarkably little difference between the sexes but there is a consistent rise in numbers of children who are home educated as ages rise. This is partly because there is a cumulative effect of children being deregistered at younger ages and remaining in home education.

It is interesting to note that many home educating families move home without informing their LEA and 'disappear' from the official statistics. This should have the effect of lowering the number of known home educated children in the older age group so the fact that this is the largest group suggests that there are even more children in this older age than the figures show. It is often claimed that children are returned to school for the purpose of taking examinations. These figures do not support this assertion. There are more than three times as many children known to be home educated by the ages of 15-16 than at the ages 5-11 when expressed as a percentage of all children of their age.

When sex and age group are considered as a percentage of all home educated children a slightly different picture emerges.

Percentage of home educated children broken down by age and sex:

	Boys	**Girls**
5-11	18.27%	14.61%
12-14	19.2%	17.78%
15-16	15.16%	15.14%

It is often assumed, from anecdotal observations of home educated children attending local groups, that home education is more popular among families with younger children. However, the researcher Leslie Barson has noted a tendency for younger families who are new to home educating to require more support and social contact with other home educating families. This suggests that younger families are over represented in local groups, giving the impression that there are more of them as a proportion of all home educated children than there really are. Furthermore, a higher percentage of all home educated children belong to the 5-11 age group it should be noted that across society as a whole there are more children of this age group.

v. De-registrations

LEAs who responded reported that there were over 3,700 de-registrations in the previous twelve months; on average more than 34 for each LEA. Extrapolating for all LEAs and school boards in the UK yields a figure of approximately 6,000 de-registrations for the purpose of home education in a given twelve month period. We cannot know how many of these families continued to home educate or how many were convinced by the LEA to return their children to school. Additionally, some parents appear to use de-registration as part of a strategy to gain a place at a school previously denied to them, so the number of ongoing home educators will be less than the de-registration figure. None the less, such a large figure represents a significant number of people involved in some form of home education. 0.07% or 7 out of every 10,000 children are deregistered from school every year for the stated intention of home education. The LEA taking part in the survey that had the greatest number of de-registrations was Kent, with 172 de-registrations in a year. Norfolk came a close second with 143 de-registrations over the previous twelve months.

vi. School Attendance Orders and Educational Supervision Orders (SAOs & ESOs)

In the UK it is the parents' responsibility to *"cause their child to receive an education suitable to his or her age, ability and aptitude and any special needs that child may have"* (Section 7 of the 1996 Education Act). LEAs may come to the view that a family is failing to provide such an education and ultimately issue a school attendance order under the provisions of the 1996 Education Act section 437. However, few of the 109 LEAs in the survey issue any SAOs at all.

Number of SAOs issued by LEAs in a twelve month period:

No. of LEAs	Number of SAOs issued	Totals
78	0	0
17	1	17
5	2	10
1	3	3
1	4	4
2	5	10
2	6	12
2	7	14
1	8	8
1	12	12
1	18	18

Total number of SAOs issued by LEAs in the survey   108

In all just 5% of the 109 LEAs were responsible for issuing 50% of the SAOs. It is hard, if not impossible, to accept that this variance could represent a real difference in parental deliverance of education in different locations. For example, Worcestershire LEA issued 18 SAOs in one year whilst Herefordshire LEA (a close neighbour, demographically similar and in fact formerly part of the same LEA) issued none. It can only be concluded that these geographic differences in issuing SAOs must be put down almost entirely to the different policies of LEAs, even to the different attitudes of individual LEA officers.

Another factor which some LEAs have reported is that SAOs require the LEA to identify a school at which the child must be enrolled. There are a number of LEAs, particularly in central London, where there are no spare places in schools. There are others where places are limited and where head teachers with almost full rolls object to taking children who they perceive as potentially problematic pupils. Consequently there are a number of LEAs in the UK who are unable or unwilling to issue SAOs as they have no school with places which could be named in the order.

What we do not know from the data is how many of these SAOs were challenged in court or how many were successful in returning a child back to school. A quirk of the legal system is that should a family be issued with an SAO and continue to refuse to enrol their child they will be taken to court for a failure to comply with the order. The family may defend the case by arguing that they are providing a suitable education 'otherwise than at school' at the time of the court case (but not necessarily at the time the order was taken out). Even if a family is found guilty (that is they haven't and enrolled the child and are judged not to be efficiently home educating) they may be fined but the order then ceases so the child may still not be enrolled in school. In short, the issuing of an SAO is far from conclusive evidence of a child being returned to school.

A question was also asked about educational supervision orders in the FOI enquiry. Put simply ESOs are used where an LEA convinces the court that parents have consistently failed to provide an education for their child. In these circumstances LEAs effectively take over the parents' 'Section 7' responsibility to provide a suitable education. ESOs are more normally used against families of children registered in school rather than home educated children, but since they have been mentioned in DfES guidance to LEAs with respect to home education they became of interest to this research. The results were comparable to those garnered on SAOs. 156 ESOs were issued by the 109 LEAs who responded but many issued none at all. Once again a small number of LEAs were responsible for a disproportionate number of such orders. Wakefield was responsible for issuing 23 ESOs a year, Oxford for 16 and Sefton for 14 (these three LEAs were, therefore, responsible for issuing one third of all ESOs in the survey for a twelve month period). Whilst there may be an element of social deprivation circumstances that might reasonably feed into the issuing of ESOs the evidence does not support any direct correlation between SAOs and social problems. Given this, it is again difficult to believe that parents in these three local authorities simply behave differently and worse in respect of their children's education than parents living elsewhere. What we are left with is the impression of a 'post code lottery' determining how the authorities will react to parents in the discharge of their duties to educate their children.

vii. Children with statements of special educational needs

Special needs statements can be applied to children diagnosed with a range of problems. A special needs child may have a specific learning difficulty, a behavioural problem, autistic spectrum disorder, language difficulty, physical disability or any other identifiable cause leading to a special requirement in educational provision. Children with special educational needs who are either enrolled at a state school or with the LEAs out of school education service (often known as Education Other than at School or 'EOTAS') should be statemented to identify their needs and how they will be fulfilled by the LEA. The provision element (section 3) of the statement can only refer to LEAs obligations. In law such statements can never place any obligation on the parents of a child.

From the wider research with families of special needs children there seems to be some level of confusion within LEAs regarding the legislation as it applies to children with special educational needs being home educated. A small minority of LEAs erroneously believe that a family needs permission to home educate a child with special needs. While this is true of a child registered at a designated 'special school' it is not generally true and even when the child is registered at a special school the LEA may not unreasonably withhold permission. An LEA should also take note of the Disabilities Discrimination Act which forbids them to discriminate between disabled children and others.

It is suspected by some families that statements are maintained as a means of placing pressure on families to allow more invasive monitoring than otherwise might take place. On the other hand some families want a Statement to be maintained to assist in maintaining other services from other agencies relating to the child's problems. The pattern of how LEAs treat Statements once a child has been de-registered varies between LEAs. Since parents are primarily responsible for their child's education then once a child is de-registered in order to home educate many LEAs will consider ceasing a statement. Others maintain Statements in order to assist in their own enquiries; they reason that if they have a Statement of the child's needs then they have something against which they can asses the parents' provision (in accordance with Section 7 of the 1996 Education Act).

From the 109 LEAs who responded to the survey there were 578 children with a statement who were being home educated, representing 0.32% of all Statements issued in those boroughs. Thus in the country over all this extrapolates to approximately 1,000 children who are being home educated and have a current Statement. It should also be remembered that not all children with special needs who are being home educated, even where those special needs have been identified and statemented in the past, have a continuing Statement. So the total number of children who are both home educated and have some special educational need will be many times this figure.

viii. Geographical distribution of home educated children with a statement

The number and geographical distribution of children with Statements of special educational needs being home educated is greatly effected by LEAs' local policies on the statementing of children. Within the survey the LEA with the largest proportion of children being home educated with a statement was York with 2.8% (19 of 687 children). This particular figure was especially remarkable in that the total proportion of children being home educated in York was a moderate 0.14%. The LEA with the greatest absolute number of children with a statement being home educated was Hampshire with 35 children, though this represents only 0.73% of all children with a statement in the LEA.

These figures once again seem to say more about differences in LEA policy towards special needs, the statementing of children, the quality of services offered to statemented children and the continuation of statements of children being home educated than they do about differences caused by geography *per se*. Twelve LEAs had no children with a statement being home educated, but remarkably three LEAs claimed not to know how many children being home educated had a statement, an admission that may represent a failure of a duty of care towards these children; without this information the LEAs in question cannot possibly develop effective policies regarding the children's' needs.

Home Educators as a Lobby

LEA data shows that there are on average 1.3 children per family being home educated. If there are 45,000 children being home educated nationally then this would give a figure of a little fewer than 35,000 families directly involved in home education, not counting grandparents, extended family etc. Earlier research suggested that over 22% of home educating families are single parents. (Fortune-Wood, 2005, p.18) From this we can determine that at least 62,500 adults are directly involved in home educating their children today.

In the US home-schoolers have been able to exert significant influence upon the political system. If home educators were evenly spread around the country then the average Member of Parliament could expect to have approximately 100 voting home educators living in his or her constituency. However, it was previously established that the distribution of home educators is uneven, with the predominant number living in the south and east of the country and generally within conurbations. This means that some MPs could expect that figure to be significantly higher.

Additionally the current phase of research indicates that the numbers of those who are home educating is growing at the rate of 17% per annum (compound). From this we can extrapolate how many people will be directly involved in home education in the future, assuming that this rate of growth is continued at similar levels (though in fact previous research indicates that the rate is likely to rise rather than decline so these figures could be under-estimated).

Estimate of numbers of children and adults involved in home education in the future	2005	2015	2025
Children home educated	45,000	216,000	1,000,000
Home educated children as a % of all children	0.56%	2.7%	12%
Children being home educated per LEA on average	265	1,300	6,100
Adults directly involved in home education	62,500	300,000	1,500,000
Home educating adults per average constituency	90	430	2,000

These projections suggest that should current rates of growth continue into the future then the social and political impact of home education could become increasingly significant. This could impact not only on electoral issues, as has been the case in the US, but also on the education industry overall. For example, this present research identifies that there are approximately 2,000 home educated children living in Kent, suggesting that there are nearly 3,000 adults directly involved in home educating their children in Kent today. By 2025 that figure could grow to 63,000 adults in Kent alone and this does not account for grandparents, those who have home educated in the past or those adults who were themselves once home educated, all of whom might feel an affinity to home education. Clearly the question 'what will education be like in twenty years time?' cannot be answered without reference to the views and interests of the growing community of home educators in the UK. Issues such as falling rolls, less need for teachers, provision of personalised education, flexi-schooling, creation of resources and/or exam centres and consideration of far more parental involvement in state provided education could all become pressing issues, some of them focused on keeping parents on board.

There are also financial implications of home education. The DfES report which deals with numbers of children in school also details the cost of a school education. The net government spending on education amounts to nearly £50. billion. The average spending on education of each child in state maintained schools is in excess of £5,500 per annum. Thus the bill for each child's compulsory school education over eleven years comes to over £60,500. With 45,000 home educators there is already a saving of over £2.7 billion over the eleven year cycle of compulsory school age. By 2025 the savings to government at current expenditure levels could grow to over £5.5 billion per annum as more parents take on this financial responsibility, in addition to which there will be infrastructure savings due to factors such as a fall in requirement for training teachers.

Part two

Support or Obstruction?

Parents who have taken the decision to retain their primary responsibility for their children's education can fare very variously depending on a number of factors. Having access to high quality information and support and to a shared pool of experience are all aspects of home education experience that can ensure social inclusion and successful educational provision. Nearly all support to home educators is undertaken by volunteers from a wide range of organisations and networks. Chapter two looks at service provision from both voluntary organisations and local education authorities. How is support provided and accessed and how is it perceived by those using it?

An ongoing issue for home educators is not only how to access support, whether formal legal advice or informal social networking, but how to deal with obstructions. Whilst there are some fine examples of bridge building between home educators and local education authorities (for example the policy arrived at in Milton Keynes through consultation with the home education community or the pro-active efforts of Bridgend LEA in supporting struggling home educators despite having no budget) there are sadly many more LEAs who place constant obstacles in the way of home educating families. Many authorities routinely persist in acting beyond the remit of their legal duties. The results of two Freedom of Information enquiries highlight a significant gap between cultures of home education and the professionals.

One of the key features of social inclusion is access to further and higher education. NFER, a supposedly 'independent' research foundation set up in 1946 to *"inform decision makers, managers and practitioners."* is undertaking research into home education which follows up an alleged DfES concern that identifies electively home educated children as a 'vulnerable group' due to lack of access to examinations at key stage 4. This of course begs the question as to why recent government policies on GCSEs have made it so difficult for home educators to access such exams. NFER's contention that home educators are vulnerable seems to rest on very tenuous grounds, including a Guardian newspaper ill-informed opinion piece article. There are many issues to address in terms of how home educated young people can access qualifications. Another element to be considered is how home educators can access university education. A chapter contributed by Jan Fortune-Wood examines admissions procedures for home educators across a sample range of arts and science disciplines.

Chapter two

Service Provision for Home Educators

The decision to home educate is one which involves parents shouldering responsibility for their children's education, a task that is normally delegated to schools. It is a task that home educators take on with significant levels of success, but clearly this can be improved and enhanced by accessing support. In addition to support services there are statutory bodies which have a role to play, albeit a limited one, and the quality of information provided and the sensitivity of interactions between parents and statutory officers are issues which impact on families' experiences of home education. There is a persistent fear of social exclusion in some perceptions of home education, a theme which will be returned to more broadly in later research, and provision of services, whether voluntary or statutory, has a role to play in ensuring social inclusion.

This part of the research was conducted via questionnaires to the home education community. The main purpose was to discover what support structures people most often use and what the perceived quality of that support is. Forty-eight families took part in this section of the research.

Diverse Support Structures

Finding quality advice and proactive support is often sighted by home educators as a significant factor in their decision making processes when first considering home educate and, later, in feeling able to continue to home educate in the longer term. Home educators have a range of issues they need to address from discovering what educational philosophy suits their particular family to finding new arenas in which they and their children can socialise; from finding their legal rights and responsibilities to how to relate to local education authority officials.

With internet availability becoming increasingly widespread more support is readily available. The speed and range of support can even be overwhelming. There are now dozens of major websites offering support, the most important of which receive in excess of two million hits per annum. There are also a wide range of internet mailing lists offering either general support to all home educators or specialist help. Examples are single parents, those with children with special needs, those who share a particular cultural or religious approach or those living within a particular locality. There are even mailing lists to support those who offer support. In addition to these support sites and list, the rise in government innovation in educational issues has resulted in the creation of a number of mailing lists that have a specifically campaigning or monitoring agenda. The number of local and national support organisations has grown with some offering telephone help-lines. Additionally LEAs may offer support in the form of website information or in their literature.

There are several major sources of support. *Education Otherwise* (EO) was founded in the 1970s by a small group of people and now with a membership well in excess of 5,500. EO is the UK's largest home education organisation with the most extensive support structure, including a network of local contacts and groups across the UK. While EO has members in Scotland, *Schoolhouse*, operating exclusively in Scotland, is dedicated to Scottish issues and support. Both of these organisations have telephone support lines, lobby government, have networks of local groups, run mailing lists, have newsletters and can offer legal support as well as other types of support to members.

The *Home Education Advisory Service* (HEAS) was created by a break away group of EO members in the mid 1990s. HEAS offers services broadly similar to those of EO. However, they far smaller than EO and maintain a slightly separatist attitude towards other activists and support groups within the home education community. The extent of their services is therefore difficult to assess.

Choice in Education is primarily a support newsletter with a website. The newsletter carries articles of interest to home educators and lists upcoming events but is largely London centric where it has its roots. The organisers are also extensively involved in other groups.

The *UK Home Education Mailing List* was established in the mid 1990s. It is the UK's oldest and most established online mailing list support for home educators. It has no website or any other structure, but has collaborated with a number of other organisations in an organic way depending upon the interests of its members. It has also engaged in important debates which have significantly influenced the outlook of home education in the UK. Its members helped to edit legal guidance on home education and have coordinated lobbying of local and national authorities. Its strength lies in its size and the experience and willingness of its members to help or become involved.

The *Home Education UK* website, originally an offshoot of the *UK Home Education Mailing List* was founded in 2000 and is run by an individual. It has a large number of web pages with articles, legal pages, and support and resource information. There are two offshoot websites; one for continental Europe and another for research. There are several mailing lists belonging to the website, some for those with special interests such as supporting families of children suffering from school phobia. The website has recently added an internet news service and a quarterly paper journal which reaches across boundaries to address home education from the perspectives of parents, academics and local education authorities. There is also a service to offer training to LEA officials in conjunction with an educationalist and practicing barrister with significant experience in home education law. The site coordinates home education community responses to government legislative and guidance reviews and receives over two million hits per annum.

There are many other relatively small specialist support groups such as those for single parents, parents of special needs children, black home educators, and those who home educate for reasons of faith. There are also a number of websites maintained by individuals some, such as *Muddle Puddle* (www.muddlepuddle.co.uk), which offers assistance to those who are home educating very young children, are of great importance to the home education community.

All in all these different resources constitute a complex web of interconnected support structures, some offering relatively comprehensive support while others concentrate on specialist issues. Individuals who see a gap in support and want to become involved tend to set up their own support and offer it to others via the existing lines of communication, either through mailing lists, websites, journals or by word of mouth.

The Quality of Support

This questionnaire began by asking people to rate the quality of the advice or support they received from some of the above organisations. There were sixteen categories and a scoring system of 1-5: 1 being very poor and 5 being excellent. The data was used to construct an overall rating. The categories were:

i. Local Contacts

While any source of support can be used to find a local contact, some sources maintain formal structures to help home educators to do this. *Education Otherwise* maintains a listing of those members who are willing to be contacted in a contact book which is part of the membership pack received by all new members of the organisation. They also try to maintain an official local contact in each LEA area who is able to offer primary assistance to all home educators in their area, and who, being a long term experienced home educator, often knows many others locally. These individuals will also often organise or help organise events in their area. This represents by far the most extensive and well organised structure to assist home educators find other families and groups close to them.

Schoolhouse maintains a similar structure in Scotland. *Choice in Education* which has a monthly newsletter and runs a website (www.choiceineducation.org.uk) publicises local groups and events around the country. This is a very useful network for those who are not members of *Education Otherwise* and can be very useful in finding local support. *Home Education UK* a large website (www.home-education.org.uk) has a webpage which lists contact individuals for regions of the UK, local mailing lists and websites for around half of all LEAs in England and Wales along side information about LEAs, their policies, websites and contact details. The *Home Education Advisory Service* can also put people in touch with local home educators; however an analysis of their support is hampered by it being exclusively available only to members.

ii. Newsletters

There are a number of newsletters offered by support organisations. EO, HEAS and *Choice in Education* are the three most widely read. The Journal *Home Education* had not begun publication at the time this survey was conducted, but already has a subscription list of around 250. At the time of writing the *Education Otherwise* newsletter with a circulation of around 5,500 is by far the largest.

iii. Legal advice,

This is a crucial category which is available in a range of forms from several parts of the network of support.

v. Locating a lawyer

In rare circumstances home educators need the services of a lawyer. However, it is recognised from the experiences of those who have used such services that few lawyers have any experience in home education law and even specialist education lawyers may not understand the complexities of how the law relates to home education since it is rare that they are asked to act in such cases. It is, therefore, crucial for families to locate someone with experience to handle their case.

v. Home education in action

Planning an alternative style of education can often be confusing for parents who are new to home education and whose only experience of education was in school. Newcomers often ask very general questions on the lines of *"what do I do?"* or *"how do I home educate?"* To answer such enquiries it is necessary to provide an insight into how people home educate in the real world, allowing newcomers to develop a picture of the range of styles of home education that are possible. This question was an attempt to determine if support services provided such an insight.

vi. Sourcing free or cheap resources

With no funding available to home educators, and with many families managing with one parent having given up work, or as single parent families, sourcing cheap and free resources is often vitally important. Indeed some families only use free, discounted or second-hand resources.

vii. Sourcing commercial learning resources

Commercial resources are most often designed for the classroom with an eye to the requirements of the National Curriculum and the key stage regime of schools. As a consequence they are often inappropriate for use in the home and, given the costs of some commercial resources, mistakes can be very expensive. Commercial companies are beginning to recognise the value of the home education market. If there are 45,000 children being home educated then even if parents spend as little as £200 per child per year on education this represents a market of £9,000,000 per annum.

Sharing information about useful and cost effective resources is common and vital throughout the home education network. Many of the resources on offer are either the same as those designed for schools or modified versions intended for home use. Few as yet produced in the UK have been primarily designed with home educators in mind, and the quality and value of what is on offer is highly variable. The additional problem that faces home educators in that few companies understand the flexible nature of home education, and so even otherwise good quality products are often disappointing as their underlying pedagogy is too restrictive.

viii. Obtaining discounts

This too can be useful and the larger organisations are sometimes able to negotiate price reductions for members or readers as part of an advertising deal. Free or discounted entry to educational venues, such as English and Welsh Heritage properties, or discounts on the cost of distance learning courses can play a valuable part in a families ability to deliver a range of educational opportunities.

ix. Help in networking with other home educators

This is one of the core activities of most home educating support groups. Parents as well as children often need to be able to find support across a broad range of boundaries. Networking not only includes local support, but virtual networks or networks developed through annual camps.

x. Exam information

Parents often say that the subject of examinations seems to creep up on them and researching the range of possibilities can be a daunting process. Home educators quickly discover that the examination system was not designed with home educators in mind, and schools are often reluctant to accept external candidates. There are ways through the system and having help with the process from other experienced home educators can be crucial to good decision making and peace of mind.

xi. Helping children to network and find contacts

By far the most frequently raised issue by those outside the home education community is that of socialisation. Most home educators do not find this to be a problem either for themselves or their children. The national network of local groups and internet structures, as well as the numerous camps and other activities serves to provide ample opportunities for children to socialise on a range of scales. It is therefore important that there are places for children to discover what is available to them.

xii. Assistance in liaising with an LEA

From time to time families can reach an impasse with their local education authority. When this happens they often need assistance from other families or support agencies, whether to clarify legal issues, give help in writing letters, provide people who will act as lay advocates to witnesses and/or record meetings etc. Being able to provide people willing and able to fulfil these roles has proved crucial to many families ongoing home education provision.

xiii. Informal social support

Parents need to socialize, and home education, like any parenting choice, is not always easy. Finding a local group is becoming easier, especially for those with internet access and for those who are members of *Education Otherwise* or *Schoolhouse* in Scotland, as there are websites which carry this information and EO provides a comprehensive local contacts list to its members. Having safe environments in which to share concerns is often crucial to home educating families.

xiv. Legislation and updates on current issues

Support networks can provide a key service by informing parents of any legislative or policy changes that effect home education. It also enables families to take part in consultations regarding possible future legislative changes.

xv. Curriculum materials

Advice on curriculum materials and their suitability to particular children and styles of education is an important aspect of support. Curriculum materials overlap with both free and commercial resources, but are also a discrete category for those families who use some measure of structured learning. Parents working on very tight budgets cannot afford to make mistakes so feedback from other home educators is often critical to their purchasing decisions. Knowing where to find feedback is therefore important.

xvi. Support in dealing with statutory agencies

Apart from dealing with local education authorities, home educators sometimes find themselves in contact with other statutory agencies. Whether it is a school at the point of de-registration, the DfES, Social Services or an official on a truancy watch scheme, it is often the case that other people have experienced similar issues in the past and can help to resolve problems.

Quality of Support with relevant mean and modal averages:

Category	Organisation	N	Range	Mean average	Modal average
local contacts	EO	31	1-5	3.7	5 (39%)
	HEAS	7	1-5	2.6	1(43%)

	C in Ed	4	1-3	3.3	
	UK H Ed	8	2-5	3.4	
	HE UK	9	3-5	4	
	Local group	18	1-5	4.5	5(72%)
	LEA	3	1-3	2	
Newsletter	eo	28	1-5	3.6	5(39%)
	heas	10	2-5	4	4(50%)
	C in Ed	10	2-5	3.7	3(40%)
	Local group	3	5	5	
legal advice	EO	20	2-5	4.1	5(45%)
	HEAS	9	3-5	4.4	5(55%)
	C in Ed	3	4	4	
	UK H Ed list	11	4-5	4.7	5(73%)
	HE UK website	12	4-5	4.8	5(83%)
	Arch	4	4-5	4.8	
locating a lawyer who under-stands HE	EO	5	1-5	3.4	
	HEAS	3	3-5	3.7	
	UK H Ed list	8	4-5	4.9	5(88%)
	HE UK website	4	3-5	4	
Examples of home education in action	EO	27	1-5	3.8	5(44%)
	HEAS	8	3-5	4.3	5(63%)
	C in Ed	7	3-5	3.9	3(43%)
	UK H Ed List	16	3-5	4.6	5(81%)
	HE UK website	10	3-5	4.5	5(70%)
	Local Groups	11	2-5	4.4	5(64%)
Sourcing free or cheap resources	EO	17	1-5	3.2	3(41%)
	HEAS	7	2-5	3.4	3(43%)
	UK h Ed list	8	2-5	3.9	5(50%)
	HE UK website	7	2-5	4	5(57%)
	Local group	11	3-5	3.9	3(45%)
Sourcing commercial learning resources	EO	12	1-5	3.6	3(42%)
	HEAS	6	2-4	3.2	4(50%)
	UK HE list	6	3-5	4.3	5(50%)

	HE UK website	4	2-4	3.3	
	Local groups	6	1-5	2.7	
Obtaining discounts	EO	20	1-5	3.5	4(40%)
	HEAS	8	3-5	3.9	
	Local Groups	7	2-5	3.3	3(43%)
Help networking with other home educators	EO	30	1-5	3.7	5(37%)
	HEAS	8	3-5	3.9	
	Cin Ed	4	3-4	3.3	3(75%)
	UK HE list	15	2-5	4.5	5(66%)
	HE UK website	6	3-5	4.7	5(83%)
	Local Groups	13	4-5	4.8	5(77%)
Exam inform-ation	EO	16	1-5	3.8	4(38%)
	HEAS	6	3-5	4.2	5(50%)
	UK HE list	10	2-5	4.3	5(50%)
	HE UK Website	8	4-5	4.6	5(63%)
	Local group	4	1-4	2.75	4(50%)
Helping children to network & find contacts	EO	18	1-5	3.7	5(44%)
	HEAS	7	1-4	2.7	
	Local Groups	13	3-5	4.7	5(82%)
Liaise on your behalf with an LEA etc.	EO	8	1-5	3.3	
	HEAS	4	2-5	3.3	3(50%)
	UK HE	3	5	5	5(100%)
	Local Groups	4	3-5	4.3	5(50%)
Informal social support	EO	18	1-5	3.5	5(39%)
	HEAS	6	2-5	3.7	
	UK HE list	13	2-5	4.5	5(62%)
	Local Groups	17	3-5	4.7	5(76%)
Legislation & issues Updates	EO	16	1-5	3.6	5(38%)
	UK HE list	11	3-5	4.6	5(73%)
	HE UK	9	5	5	5(100%)
	HEAS	6	4-5	4.8	5(83%)
	Local Groups	5	1-5	3.2	3(40%)
	Arch	3	3-5	4	

Curriculum materials	EO	11	1-5	2.6	1(36%)
	HEAS	4	3-4	3.3	3(75)
	Local Groups	5	1-5	2.6	
Support in dealing with statutory agencies	EO	13	1-5	3	1(31%)
	HEAS	5	2-5	3.4	
	CinEd	3	3	3	3(100%)
	UK HE list	8	4-5	4.5	
	HE UK website	6	4-5	4.7	5(67%)
	Local Groups	7	2-5	4	5(43%)

(The over all N figure represents the total number of entries for each category and includes a number of organisations which had too few entries to be of any significance)

Extrapolating average ratings on quality of service

Having collated scores for the separate categories of service delivery a question arose about the overall scores achieved by each of the sources of support. One way to assess the quality of services provided by various groups or services is to simply list them in order of the overall average score. As below:

Organisation	n	Mean
Schoolhouse	16	4.9
FRED	13	4.7
Fluff List	7	4.7
UK HE	126	4.4
HE UK	87	4.3
Arch Ed	14	4.2
Local Groups	72	4.1
HEAS	102	3.8
Home Service	17	3.7
Muddle Puddle	12	3.7
EO	283	3.6
Choice in Ed	48	3.3
LEAs	22	1.9

However, this method ignores the fact that some organisations deal with many times the work load of others. *Education Otherwise* for example has around 5,500 members and is many times the size of the next organisation down in size. This is generally reflected in the number of people who identified each structure in reply to my questions. It would probably be unfair not to take this into account, so the same table could also be ranked meaningfully by n (the sample size for each support group). This would indicate the score by sample size as below:

Organisation	n	Mean
EO	283	3.6
UK HE	126	4.4
HEAS	102	3.8
HE UK	87	4.3
Local Groups	72	4.1
Choice in Ed	48	3.3
LEAs	22	1.9
Home Service	17	3.7
Schoolhouse	16	4.9
Arch	14	4.2
FRED	13	4.7
Muddle Puddle	12	3.7
Fluff List	7	4.7

This table suggests that the best support overall seems to come from smaller groups. Despite this the largest groups, like *Education Otherwise*, achieve an overall mean average of fair to good. In fact only LEAs taken as a whole score less than fair. Probably largely because too frequently the quality of the legal information they run on their websites is incorrect, and they often fail to offer information or support of any other kind. It appears that LEAs do not offer much of benefit to home educators and what they do offer is often incorrect. However, it should be noted that there are a few LEAs who make a positive effort to offer what help and support they can, often on a very limited or even non existent budget.

Local groups are unsurprisingly good at supporting people on a local level while being poor at dealing with larger issues such as sourcing commercial resources or locating legal advice since their membership base is too small.

On the other hand, one of the problems that the larger groups face is that the support their volunteers can provide can be extremely variable. EO particularly suffers from this problem. While their average quality of support was rated above fair, the range of responses which mentioned them was quite large. In looking at the modal average (the most frequently given score value), EO was largely rated as good to excellent, but in two categories EO only scored 1; one of these categories being the often crucially important one of providing support with dealing with statutory agencies. In another part of the survey a parent highlighted this problem saying:

> *"The EO contact told me she was too busy to deal with me and did not suggest anyone else."*

It would seem that while many of *Education Otherwise's* volunteers do an excellent job in dealing with enquiries, a small number of those seeking help do not find the assistance they need. From this it would appear that consideration should be given to improving training and or the selection of volunteers.

Crucial Resources

Open-ended and qualitative questions yielded far more detailed information. For example, one question asked what people regarded as their most important resources. I expected answers associated with particular groups or structures but of the 41 responses to this question the most frequently mentioned reply (25) was the crucial importance of the emotional support gained from friends, family and other home educators, either locally or online in virtual groups.

The next most frequently mentioned (14) source of support was legal support, particularly from those online groups that engage in this kind of help. Drafting reports, writing letters and formulating complaints were frequently needed sources of support. Others mentioned the need to identify experienced lawyers in situations where an LEA had issued a school attendance order or, less frequently, a Social Services department, often ignorant of the basic legality of home education, attempts to bring an action on the spurious grounds of social isolation. The other issue of importance relating to the law is that of monitoring legislative change. Besides the large organisations such as *Education Otherwise* and smaller dedicated groups like *Arch Ed* (Action on the Rights of Children in Education) who monitor legislation in the area of education for both home educated and school going children, there are also key individuals with no formal training who have never the less built up considerable expertise in monitoring government white and green papers, proposed legislation and guidance documents. Such people are invaluable to the community in guarding against changes that could negatively impact on home education.

Another frequently mentioned source of support was charity shops, scrap stores and other facilities not part of the home education community, but none the less important in providing facilities or resources to families. Without these sources of materials the cost of educating at home would be considerably more. One parent listed key resources as:

> *"Sympathetic childcare for short period each week; knowing that others are keeping an eye on legislation, case law and our right to home educate; other families locally to share time and activities with; grandparents who don't interfere and can be supportive; the scrap store, charity shops, cheap bookshops etc."*

Support at the Beginning of Home Education

The next three questions related to families who were just beginning to home educate: Did you need support? Did you get support? Did you pay for support?

Some families begin to home educate and have no problems. Others find it more difficult to adjust to home education and some have prolonged difficulties with their LEA. So, if new families felt that they needed support, how easy it was to find and did they find it necessary to used paid-for support.

The results were:

	Yes	No
Did you need support?	42	5
Did you get support?	40	3
Did you pay for support?	7	35

Clearly many of those who needed support and did not get it would not appear in this survey as many of them would have given up home educating. However, 6% of those who continued to home educate failed to find the support they needed when they first began to home educate. Other research suggests that the 'failure' rate among those de-registering to home educate could be as high as 75% in the first year, though it is probable that many of these never intended to continue to home educate into the long- term. This would be an interesting and important area for further research but since it would require detailed access to personal records held by LEAs it is not likely to be feasible research, and it is difficult to determine the real picture on the level of success support structures can achieve across all those de-registering in any twelve month period.

Seven (15%) of respondents felt the need to pay for support to enable them to successfully begin to home educate. If this is an accurate portrayal of the real situation it could mean that several hundreds of parents a year are paying to get support that is freely available if only they knew where to look. This is an unfortunate state of affairs given that the majority of home educating parents are already suffering financially from their decision to de-register their children. Furthermore, it reflects badly on LEAs who are well aware of the major support providers and could easily direct new parents to free sources of good quality advice and support. Notwithstanding this, the vast majority (74%) of those who continued to home educate did find the support they needed without having to pay for it, and another 11% did not feel the need to seek support in the first place.

Forty-one families agreed to provide further details on the support they received when starting out, each typically identifying several sources of assistance. It seems that EO is by far the organisation responsible for most support for those beginning to home educate. Twenty-seven families found support there. EO was frequently able to provide some free legal advice and the name of a local contact (the organisation currently has a network of around 100 local contacts). Eighteen families received advice from another home educating individual, usually someone local to them and often acting independently and on their own initiative. Six families identified their local group as a source of early support, particularly in the form of more experienced families who were willing to support them. The independent online sources seem not to feature so large in supporting those who are new to home education. The *Home Education UK* website (www.home-education.org.uk) was referred to by name only six times and the UK Home Ed mailing list only twice. This suggests that these online resources are more frequently found later on. However, those who reported finding these resources at an early stage were delighted with the results. HEAS, while receiving praise from those who used it, only received 3 comments.

While the majority of responses were positive, the quality of support does seem to vary widely.

"Education Otherwise newsletter was effective, accurate, friendly, informative."

There were a small number who found problems with support received from the larger organisations. Clearly there is a limit to what volunteers can be expected to provide before overload impacts upon their ability to offer a service. EO itself has grown from just 1,500 members in the mid 1990s to 5,500 in 2006. The support structure has been improved with attention to the telephone help-line and the employment of a membership secretary, but otherwise the organisation remains substantively the same today, with the additional workload of thousands of extra members and the enquiries they generate.

Support from Local Education Authorities

LEAs offered praiseworthy assistance to only two families:

> *"The LEA has a department for elective home education and they have been very helpful."*

More often LEAs were cited as the source of problems for which the family then needed advice.

> *"...gave much support and helped with LEA who were being very difficult"*

Few LEAs have specialist, dedicated departments dealing with electively home educating families. It was noticeable that one of the two positive comments came from one of those rare LEAs where a dedicated home education department existed. The common practice is to tack home education onto the end of a long list of other responsibilities. It is typical to find that the department dealing with home education is something like "the attendance department" or "education inclusion unit" or even "behavioural support". This leads to several consequences that cause problems to home educating families.

Firstly, it means that LEA officers are rarely trained in the specific issues of home education. It is rare to find an LEA which has a thorough understanding of the legal aspects of home education. During 2005 Clare Murton undertook a review of online LEA policies to assess the quality of LEA legal understanding. Of the seventy-five LEAs which have their policy online only one (Milton Keynes) has been found to have a policy that suggests a thorough understanding of the legislation.

In departments where the officers are primarily concerned with issues of attendance or educational welfare it is quite likely that they will see their primary aim as being to return children to school. If the department is one that mostly deals with problem families then parents are concerned that they too will be seen as a problem and that this will lead to an unfavourable assessment of their provision. This often leads to conflict between the family and the LEA.

Another problem is that although LEAs often talk about developing an ongoing relationship with families this is logistically difficult when staff change from one year to the next and cases are distributed among a number of officers who may or may not have any experience of home education. As a consequence of this families never know who they are dealing with or whether the officer has any understanding of how home education works.

Drafting Letters

Many families have problems with drafting letters to the LEA. They may lack the confidence or the technical skills required to express themselves clearly. Assistance with letter writing is therefore a major element of support provision.

Twenty-two families said that they needed help with drafting a letter while twenty-six did not. Of those who did need help with this only one failed to find it and none paid for it. In all cases people were happy with the result. Typically people found a pro forma or example letter, more often than not on the internet, and then edited it with help from either one of the formal support groups or from other local home educating families. The quality of support in this area seems good.

Ongoing and General Support

As families continue to home educate they often need longer term, general advice. Nine families came into this group. Of these all but one found the support they needed, though one of these had to pay for it.

There followed a series of questions about the provision of general support, which people were asked to simply agree or disagree with.

Only seven people (15%) agreed to the proposition that information and support was fragmentary or of poor quality. Rather more people (35%) felt that the quality of support and information varied enormously and the same number felt that support groups were hampered in delivering support by internal politics. (It would be surprising, given the diversity of outlook between home educators, if there was not a degree of disagreement between various parts of the home education community in how best to proceed on issues.)

On the subject of accurate legal advice 19% felt with that legal advice was sometimes inadequate or inaccurate. Overall only 26 respondents (54%) of people felt that there was plenty of good quality support for anyone who wants it. Given that the major support organisation has been in existence for over twenty-five years this is perhaps a rather disappointing figure.

Diversity

Just as the home education community itself is diverse, so too is the support that is on offer. Many of the differing home educating 'outlooks' have support groups or structures which reflect their views and this results in a highly complex network. Those new to home education inevitably find this rather confusing. Eight families (17%) agreed with the proposition that there is a need for an improvement in dialogue between support structures with the aim of clarifying the situation. Whilst only 5 families (10%) felt that there was too much duplication of support, 37 families (77%) felt that having a wide range of sources of support enables people to find the most appropriate services for their needs, indicating that people value the range and variety of support on offer. This correlates with the finding that only eight families (17%) felt that accessing support is confusing because there are so many competing sources of information.

Nearly half of all those who responded to the questionnaire agreed that there needs to be a gateway that brings together different advice services. It is interesting to note that there are in fact already gateways, such ε ` the support page of the *Home Education UK* website and the *Home Education UK* web-ring, but the fact that people feel the need for a gateway may indicate that they find it difficult to locate or do not realise that they exist. It might also be that they are not regarded as sufficiently comprehensive.

Making contact with home educators who do not have internet access is a more intractable problem. Cooperation with the media has been the favoured method to date as this can generate free publicity, which is important given that home educators do not have any budget for advertising. Although making contact with new home educators is an ongoing issue thirty two families (67%) felt that it should not be left to the state to provide information as they felt it too often came with an agenda. Interestingly, although the DfES have a number of portals on the internet offering advice to parents considering home educating not one parent mentioned using this resource. On the other hand, several families did use LEAs as a source of information.

There is persistent anecdotal evidence that home educators tend to be highly independent minded and more than usually self-reliant. I asked respondents whether they thought that is should be the responsibility of individual families to find any support that they need for themselves. Twenty families (42%) in the survey agreed that it was up to individual families to fulfil their own needs for dealing with any problems that they encountered.

Finally, in this series of questions families were asked if they would be prepared to pay commercial rates for high quality, professional support. Only three families agreed to this probably reflecting the lower than average incomes for many home educators. (Fortune-Wood, 2005, pp. 22-23).

Attitudes Towards State Involvement in Home Education

The final part of this survey looked at state provision. It has long been an issue for the home education community whether or not to campaign for financial assistance with home education. Home educators undoubtedly pay taxes like everyone else and the education budget is a major destination for those taxes, amounting to around £50 billion in 2005 or approximately 5,500 for every child of compulsory school age in the UK. Many home educators understandably resent the fact that they have no access to any of this funding when it comes to providing an education to their children.

The problem for many, however, is that it is well understood that should the government contribute to the cost of home education then the Auditing Commission, in the form of OFSTED, would soon pay a more than passing interest in home education. It is reasoned by many home educators that the government would soon insist on parents adopting the National Curriculum or perhaps a cut down version of it, as is the case in some other parts of the world, as a mandatory requirement, and that mandatory monitoring and testing could follow hard on the heels of accessing public funds.

Despite this many home educators still hold the view that the state should financially support home educators. In the survey 24 families (50%) agreed with the statement that the state should offer grants in the form of either vouchers or money for home education. Interestingly, Conservative Party policy in 2004 suggested something similar by proposing that parent led and other small independent schools should be able to receive £5,000 grants from the government for each child enrolled, though it was unclear at the time if this would extend to parents educating their children at home.

Despite the support for grants and the risk of much heavier monitoring that such funding would bring with it, only six families thought that the LEA should have a role in assessing educational provision. This strongly suggests that many home educators have either not considered the full implication of receiving grants or have discounted the risk. Anecdotal evidence suggests that families who are relatively new to home education are more likely to want funding, whilst more experienced home educators realise that the loss of independence would be an unacceptable price to pay for grants.

A related issue to monetary support is having access to teacher resources and equipment. Most LEAs have teacher resource centres where teachers can obtain resources and small items of equipment either for free or for a fee paid by their school. Some LEAs have in the past offered access to these resources to home educating parents in their area though this seems to be becoming less frequent. Thirty families (63%) agreed that this would be a useful facility and a further 19 (40%) thought that LEAs should offer curriculum information or advice. Similarly 36 families (75%) believed that access to library facilities should be widened for home educators. In many areas (for example Birmingham) extended borrowing rights or internet access is already available by the simple mechanism of allowing home educators to register with the library under the same conditions as a local community group. This gives home educators extended loans of books and other materials, making educational planning and implementation far more simple and also taking away the constant threat of library fines.

Families were asked about the idea of using library services as a key provider of information on home education. Thirty one families (65%) believed that library services could become a key source of information. Libraries are generally thought of as neutral ground between LEAs and families, they are sometimes used as alternative venues for meeting LEA officers, they are located in most areas and the flexible ethos of research-based education is one more attuned to that of most home educators' philosophies. Still on the issue of information dissemination, 33 families (69%) agreed that it was the business of the state to offer information on parental rights and 35 families (73%) wanted LEAs to put them in touch with local and national home education support services.

Examinations can be an area of contention for home educators, particularly in terms of access and cost. The cost of taking GCSEs examinations as an external candidate can be high (Fortune-Wood, 2005, p.19) and taking several exams can be financially out of reach for some parents. In addition, it is often difficult to find schools which will accept external candidates.

Forty-two families (88%) felt that LEAs could do more in ensuring that there was access for external candidates to take exams and 32 families (67%) thought that LEAs should cover the costs of the invigilation and exam fees for external candidates.

There followed a series of five questions relating to rights and duties in terms of both LEAs and home educators. The second sentence of Article 2 Protocol 1 of the European Convention on Human Rights says:

> "...the State shall respect the right of parents to ensure such education and teaching is in conformity with their own religious and philosophical convictions."

This statement should form the basis of any assessment of provision made by home educators (Fortune-Wood, 2006, p.4) but while some local authorities have understood this many others have not. Many LEAs still seek to prescribe what parents can teach their children by determining beforehand what they regard as being an adequate, or suitable education. (See Chapter Three) Doncaster and Nottinghamshire LEAs for example have a list of subjects that must be taught:

> "English, Mathematics, Science, Information and Communications Technology (ICT) and opportunities for physical, social, spiritual and cultural development."

While some items of these supposedly 'essential requirements' may seem non-contentious, others, such as information technology is highly problematic for those belonging to some religious groups who object to computers and, in any case, it is up to parents to devise an education for their children. The only legal requirements are that it should be efficient (i.e. achieve what it sets out to achieve), and suitable (i.e. fits the child for life in his or her particular cultural group).

In addition, the law of evidence is such that home educators may provide evidence in any form they wish, despite which some local authorities insist that only certain forms of evidence are acceptable. Southend-on-Sea, for example, require home visits, marked work, and access to the child; none of which they are able to demand in law. (See Chapter Three)

When asked, forty-two families (88%) of home educators believe that LEAs should respect the diversity of educational provision and evidence of education, and forty-two families (92%) want LEAs to respect their rights to a private family life. Similarly, twenty-nine families (60%) want LEAs to strictly adhere to their minimum legal duties in regard to home education.

A function often demanded by LEAs (which they currently do not have) is that of ensuring that all home educated children within an LEA are known and registered. This demand received almost no support from those who responded to the survey, with only three families (6%) agreeing. The question whether child welfare considerations necessitate that other statutory agencies, such as social services, should become key providers of support to home educators, received no support at all.

The Quality of Information Provided by LEAs

During 2005 Clare Murton undertook a review of online guidance to parents provided by local education authorities. There are approximately 150 LEAs in England and around eighty of them mention elective home-based education on their websites. The review of web content on home education was primarily an attempt to rate the quality of the advice given by LEAs to home educators, particularly the legal advice being offered on their websites. Many LEAs do not make this information available online and the work has also been supplemented by written requests for LEA policy statements.

Generally local authority websites are difficult to navigate and often hold the information in pdf files, which is useful for printing, but less friendly to view online as they take longer to download and require additional software to read. Only one website, Milton Keynes, presents an extensive policy that has no legal errors or apparent attempts to mislead readers. The remainder suffer from two broad kinds of problem. They either make statements that are simply wrong in law, with demands on families that are legally insupportable or they mislead people into thinking that they have powers that they do not in fact have by a literary slight of hand. A good example of the latter is that of the Parent Centre website run by the Department of Education and Skills. This website states that a local authority:

"may ask to visit the family home to talk to the parent and child, and to look at examples of work".

The next paragraph correctly states,

"Local Authorities have no automatic right of access to parents' homes."

but goes on to say

"Parents may wish to offer an alternative way of demonstrating that they are providing suitable education, for example through showing examples of work and agreeing to a meeting at another venue."

Parents could easily form the view from this that although they can refuse a home visit they must then have a meeting and show samples of the child's work, neither of which are true. The LEA has no rights to prescribe how parents present information.

Misapplications of the law are frequent and regular on LEA websites. It seems that many LEAs use each others' policies re copied from one LEA to another and so perpetuating errors. The most typical errors include:

i. Home visits.

Many local authorities expect home visits as standard and will push very hard to have them. They sometimes believe that Section 175 of the 2002 Education Act empowers them to make such demands, but this section simply places a duty upon LEAs to have a general care for the welfare of children in any function they already exercise and plainly does not confer any right of entry to private homes.

ii. Broad and balanced

The term 'broad and balance' arises in Section 9 of the 1996 Education Act and refers specifically to pupils who must, according to the section, receive a broad and balanced education. However, under the Act a pupil is defined as a child of compulsory educational age who attends an institute of learning, which cannot in law describe a home. Therefore, there is no requirement in law for parents to provide a broad and balanced education, only one that is suitable to the individual child under Section 7 of the same Act. A booklet produced by Cambridgeshire LEA wrongly states that home educated children *"should receive a good, broad, balanced curriculum appropriate to their individual needs"*. It goes on to say that such an education should include various parts of the National Curriculum, which has absolutely no legal application to home educators.

iii. Ongoing monitoring

It is almost universally assumed by local authorities that families should be subjected to ongoing monitoring. The legal framework for LEA duties are exclusively laid out in section 437 of the 1996 Education Act where there is no mention of monitoring, only a duty to act if the LEA have actual cause for believing that no education is taking place. There is no duty to inspect a family where *"there is no appearance of no education taking place"*. The ignorance of the law within education authorities and government departments is so widespread that even the DfES schools minister Jacqui Smith insists, quite wrongly, in a letter to me dated 17 April 2006 that, *"local authorities have a general duty to ensure that all children in their area are receiving a suitable full time education"*. This is legally untrue, there is simply no such duty, and when asked to cite such law MS Smith has failed to reply.

iv. De-registration

De-registration is a right in law in England and Wales and may not be denied unless the child is attending a special school and has been since the current Pupil Registration Regulations were passed in 2005, (even then permission to home educate cannot be unreasonably denied). However, there are still local authorities who seem not to have realised this. Bury LEA until mid May 2006 had a flow chart of actions to be taken should a child be de-registered. The key element of this chart was a box that said *"Parents must satisfy the LEA that their arrangements are suitable **before** the child's name can be taken off the register"*.

Similarly Cambridge LEA say: *"Should the LEA officer be satisfied that you have demonstrated that your child is receiving suitable education he/she will write to you notifying you of this. Should your child be registered at a special school, the LEA will advise the school to remove your child's name from the school roll"*. Cambridge state that this is the end point of their deregistration procedure which, by the LEA's own admission, can easily take two months or more. This form of procedure is not only a mis-statement of the law, but if a school followed the LEA's advice and delayed de-registration then the head teacher could be personally prosecuted under criminal powers contained in Section 9 of the Pupil Registration Regulations 1995. To be compliant with the law, de-registration should be immediate upon receiving written notification that a child is being home educated and the LEA should be informed within 10 working days by the head teacher that this has happened.

v. Statements of Special Educational Need

Statements of Special Educational Need make no difference to the procedures (though attendance at a designated special school does). Some LEAs like Dorset believe that such statements obligate parents in some way. Cambridge insists that those children with (or who are suspected of having) special needs require different procedures for de-registration: *"Should your child have special educational needs it is important that you have a full and open discussion with LEA staff before you make any decision about home education".* They go on to say that *"When a child with a statement is home educated, parents are still obliged to adhere to the provisions of the statement".* This is absolutely not the case. Only an LEA can be made to act upon the provisions of a Statement of Special Educational Needs; these can never apply to parents. Further to this, they add that if the child is registered at a special school she *"cannot be removed from the roll of that school without the agreement of the LEA".* While this is technically correct, the LEA cannot unreasonably refuse to de-register the child and the onus would be on the LEA to show that their refusal to de-register is reasonable.

Some LEAS, like Bournemouth and Southend, confuse elective home education with what is known as EOTAS, (Education other than at school). This provision may sound like the same thing, but has a totally different legal basis, referring to children who do not have a school place, but for whom the LEA has educational responsibility (sick children, children in authorities with insufficient school places, excluded children etc). This is for children who are registered with a school but cannot for one reason or another attend. The two terms should not be confused as the LEA duties are quite different to those for electively home educated children. Sometimes the confusion arises because the same team who work with children and families under the EOTAS banner also work with electively home educated children.

Chapter three

A View from
Local Education Authorities

An Agenda Gap?

It is frequently noted by both home educators and local education authority personnel that the relationship between parents and government officers can be an uneasy one, The legal remit of LEAs towards home educators is based on only limited sections of the 1996 Act (Section 7 and Section 437) and is framed in the negative. Section 437 is clearly written in two parts – **if** (and only if), it appears to an LEA that no suitable education is taking place, **then** they can ask for evidence of educational provision. It is rare to find an LEA that follows this two stage procedure, or even one that has noticed the existence of this two phase enquiry. The first part requiring only informal sifting, not evidence as such, and the second part requiring evidence only in cases where there is an appearance of no education. Even at this stage there is no remit for the LEA to prescribe what form of evidence parents can choose to offer, and parents only need to show evidence that would convince a reasonable person that on the balance of probabilities only that a suitable education is taking place.

Given the slight nature of LEA duties in law towards home educators this might seem to be a straightforward relationship, but this is often not the case, and this has not been helped by the plethora of welfare legislation which officers are often unsure of how and whether to apply to home educators. Very few LEA personnel enter posts with outright animosity towards home educators (though there are exceptional cases of individuals who are clearly on a mission to return every child to school). What is more frequently the case, is that there is a misunderstanding of the role of the LEA sometimes accompanied by particular conceptions of education, sometimes exacerbated by particular conceptions of what kind of parents are 'capable' of home educating and often made worse by confusing educational choices with child welfare issues.

Nearly all local education authorities strongly favour, if not expect, to be able to visit parents and children in their homes at least annually, and nearly always they see this as evidence gathering (jumping straight to the second limb of Section 437) and not as a simple sifting process to gain a view that there is not an appearance of no education taking place. In the face of increasing resistance to home visits from home education support networks and many individual home educators, the response is often that the local education authority sees itself as promoting a partnership with parents, as being supportive of parents right to home educate, interested in the education taking place and free of any value judgements about particular lifestyles or educational philosophies and styles. Despite this, the actions of LEAs, as opposed to what is said, can often appear to home educators to be negative, critical and undermining. There is often a gap between what is said and what home educators experience, and the content of this gap and the hidden agendas it might hide have never before been explored in home education research.

An opportunity to redress this situation came in 2005 when the DfES published a draft of their guidelines to LEAs on home education. This draft was the latest in a series of attempts to rewrite the guidance dating back several years, previous attempts having come to grief as a result of staff changes. One previous draft, produced late in 2004 and containing serious legal errors, met fatal opposition from the home education community when it was inadvertently leaked.

This latest 2005 version combined the well received work of the Scottish Executive on guidance to school boards with elements from earlier DfES drafts and some new material. Home educators and lawyers involved in responding to the draft generally found it to be repetitive and still legally inaccurate, partly because of the differing legal situation in Scotland and partly because the drafters of the guidelines had an inadequate understanding of the law as it relates to home education.

The drafting was followed by a consultation period during which interested parties were able to submit responses to the DfES for consideration in further redrafting of the guidance. Once the consultation process had closed the DfES was approached in February of 2006, using the Freedom of Information Act to obtain all the consultation returns sent to them. The consultation provided an excellent opportunity to obtain the uncensored views of local authorities (and others) regarding home education, particularly as it is unlikely that those who made submissions would have anticipated the FOI enquiry. While the DfES were willing to provide these documents, it required an exchange of emails and a complaint to the information commissioner before they were passed on with their headers intact. It was only with this vital information that it was possible to identify which document had emanated from which local authority, or indeed, if the document emanated from a local authority at all. It was not necessary to know the identity of individual authors as these were not the target of the investigation; therefore this information was blanked out.

The documents ran to over 600 pages and included responses from HEAS, EO, the *Family Trust*, myself, two anonymous individuals, twenty-two LEAs and three joint submissions from LEA 'clusters' representing the north east of England; the south west of England and North London boroughs. The LEA responses varied enormously from short two page documents to huge documents. Some simply raised one or two points while others attempted to re-write or overwrite the original document.

DfES Draft Consultation Document for Guidance to LEAs in England 2005.

The DfES draft contained a number of legal errors which home educators identified in their responses. Of major concern were the following errors and misunderstandings.

The draft relied heavily upon the use of section 9 of the 1996 Education Act which says:

> *"In exercising or performing all their respective powers and duties under the Education Acts the Secretary of State local education authorities and the funding authorities shall have regard to the general principle that pupils are to be educated in accordance with the wishes of their parents, so far as that is compatible with the provision of efficient instruction and training and the avoidance of unreasonable public expenditure."*

Section 9 refers exclusively to 'pupils' which is defined in Section 3 of the 1996 Education Act as being *"a person for whom education is being provided at a school"*. This section, therefore, cannot apply to home educated children as a home cannot be a school. This basic error, which has been discussed on numerous occasions with the DfES and other bodies, led to a number of other subsequent problems throughout the guidance.

The first serious error of thinking that arises from this misapplication of Section 9 is that there is a statutory relationship between parents and LEAs;

which there is not. Other than the limited powers laid out in Section 437 of the same act which provides a duty for an LEA to act only if there is cause for them to believe that no education is taking place. This error is made explicit in paragraph 2.3 of the guidance (see Appendix 1) which clearly states that the local education authority has a responsibility to ensure an adequate provision for education because of Section 9 duties and that this brings the parents and the LEA into a statutory relationship. Since Section 9 does not apply this is simply incorrect. This fatally flaws the whole guidance since section 4 of the document, the details of the relationship LEAs should develop with home educating parents, takes paragraph 2.3 as its premise, leaving the essential Part 4 of the guidance based on the DfES's faulty interpretation of Section 9, which cannot be applied to home educated children.

In paragraph 2.9 the guidance recognises that Section 175(1) of the Education Act 2002 to safeguard and promote the welfare of children, does not in fact confer any new powers on LEAs. Despite this the guidance states that the LEA has a duty to follow a multi-agency approach in pursuit of S 175 (1) which, if followed, would lead to serious breaches of the Data Protection Act. Only where the LEA has reason to believe that a child is at risk of immediate and significant harm can it legitimately involve other bodies. This theme is taken up again later in paragraph 4.11 where the DfES discusses the issue of child protection and the sharing of information between agencies, again assuming duties which do not exist.

Moving on to Section 3 of the guidelines, which deals with clear policies and procedures, paragraph 3.9 of the draft uses the term 'proposals' in the context of de-registration from school to home educate. This suggests that de-registration is subject to review by the LEA, which is not the case; withdrawal to home educate is normally a right in law and not subject to the consent of the LEA.

Paragraph 3.10 is highly self contradictory. It discusses cases where there is 'cause for concern' over a withdrawal to home educate and states that former 'irregular attendance' at school is not a cause for concern, but then lists cases where there have been 'condoned' absences or truancy as being causes for concern.

Paragraph 3.12 attempts to turn a right into an obligation by saying that case law will *"require home educators to have some kind of philosophy, approach or framework..."* While parents may have such a philosophy and might be wise to do so there is no *obligation* for them to have one in law.

Paragraphs 3.15 and 3.16 take this further by attempting to limit the range of acceptable philosophical approaches open to home educators. The list of educational criteria which an LEA might 'reasonably' be expected to see include not only a philosophy, but also individual resources that are contrary to some educational philosophies (e.g. home educating families who follow Plymouth Brethren beliefs do not have computers for religious reasons so listing ICT resources immediately puts them into a category that would give 'concern'). There is no such thing in law as a 'list' which if not ticked off requires LEA officers to investigate.

Paragraph 3.18 contradicts paragraph 3.10 which correctly *states "there is no express requirement in the 1996 Education Act for LEAs to actively investigate whether parents are complying with their duties"*. Paragraph 3.18, on the other hand, *says "The frequency with which an authority will wish to contact parents to discuss their ongoing home education provision will vary..."* and goes on to say that it is up to the LEA to decide how often to make enquiries.

The guidance then moves on to School Attendance Orders (SAOs) in 3.19, suggesting that a failure to provide an education which fits any of its invented criteria listed in paragraph 3.15, may lead the LEA to 'reasonably' seek entry to the home. Paragraph 3.19 goes on to suggest that a refusal by the parents to allow access to the home could lead to the LEA issuing a SAO. Not only is there no provision for allowing entry to the home other than in 'exceptional circumstances' but it should also be noted that the list of criteria in paragraph 3.15 is arbitrary and has no legal standing.

One of the most serious errors in the document is contained in paragraph 3.20 which argues that it would be legitimate for an LEA to consider a care order where an SAO has been issued and parents continue to refuse to register their child at school. This constitutes a serious breach of due legal process. The only proper recourse for the LEA where an SAO is issued and the child is not subsequently registered at school is to prosecute the parents for failure to comply with the order. The parent then has the opportunity to defend the case by demonstrating to the court that he or she is providing an education at home. It is interesting to note that at this stage the court will not require access to the home or require that it sees the child; neither will it prescribe what the parent can offer as evidence. Even if the parents are guilty of not providing a suitable education at home, neglect of education is not in law a welfare concern of itself, it is an educational issue and it is not legitimate for the LEA to abuse Educational Supervision Orders in order to supplant the role of the parents until and unless all other legal avenues have been exhausted.

Turning to Part 4, Developing Relationships, paragraph 4.11 puts the LEA into a proactive position by wrongly stating that they have a duty to *"assure themselves of the quality of education received by children educated at home"*. There is no such duty. The law provides for an evidential stage only when there is an appearance of no suitable education taking place.

The LEA Responses

It is interesting to note that not one LEA raised objections to the errors found by home educators and lawyers. Whether this was because LEAs do not themselves understand the legal position or because they were happy to work with these errors is not known, but it is certainly the case that most LEAs who responded to the DfES consultation wanted to go even further than the DfES guidance in extending *ultra vires* powers.

In analysing the responses from local education authorities the focus is on the main themes raised by the consultation responses with highlighted examples of each issue. Interestingly, many responses did not engage with the guidance at all, but were written as emotive pleas for increased legal powers to investigate and prosecute home educators. That said, there were also a small minority of submissions that showed positive and enlightened attitudes.

i. Child protection

Principle among the issues raised by LEAs was the lack of their right to see the child. The submission from the North and East London cluster began their submission with this issue and quoted Section 175(1) of the 2002 Education Act.

> *"A local education authority shall make arrangements for ensuring that the functions conferred on them in their capacity as a local education authority are exercised with a view to safeguarding and promoting the welfare of children"*

The submission went on to say that in order to meet the requirements of this section LEAs must have access to home educating children. In fact Section 175 (1) does not mention special access to pro-actively investigate welfare issues where there is no reason to suspect or imagine a problem. Section 175(1) is a repeat of existing duties and does not confer any new powers or duties on LEAs. In particular it does not confer any rights, duties or powers to visit a child where no prior concern exits; the thrust of this section is that welfare should be taken into account during the course of exercising existing duties, not that it should create new duties.

Parent's rights to a private family life are protected by Article 8 of the European Convention on Human Rights as incorporated into the Human Rights Act. Although this does allow the State to over-ride this right where there are genuine welfare concerns, it does not allow the State the right to proactively seek out concerns or to investigate where there is no pre existing cause to be concerned. No act of parliament can overturn this right as European law has primacy, and the UK is a signatory to the European Convention on Human Rights.

It seems to be a common error by LEAs that they have a duty to proactively seek access to children to determine whether their welfare is at risk merely on the grounds that they are being educated at home. If this were true it would fundamentally alter the relationship between state and family, turning officers of the State into inspectors in family homes with the right of access with no more reason than state officials had not seen the child recently. This clearly undermines the primacy of the family and the privacy of individuals, it would bring about a police state with the absolute right of entry to a persons' home without the need for good cause. Home education is not a *prima facie* cause for concern, any more than a parent caring for a child under five and not yet at school is regarded as a *prima facie* welfare problem.

Newham said in their submission:

> "Children who attend school, can be seen by professionals, such as the education welfare service to ensure that children are not subject to abuse or neglect."

North Yorkshire said:

> "if parents persistently deny the LEA access to their home and/or child it will be more difficult to fulfil the LEA's responsibility in relation to Safeguarding Children"

And Surrey said:

> "the LEA [is] required to see home educated children and young people at least every six months".

Of course, the LEA has no such right of access and there is no such 'requirement'. Such comments clearly infer that parents are not to be trusted with their children and that the state must have access to all children in order to protect them from their parents. North Lincoln LEA actually went as far as to state what others hinted at. In section 4.8 where the guidance from the DfES says, *"where a parent elects not to allow access to their home or their child this does not of itself constitute a ground for concern about the education provision being made..."* the LEA commented, *"we feel it should!"* and further more objected strongly to the idea that evidence could be offered in any other form. North Lincoln took the particularly harsh view that because there were no extant concerns about a family this did not mean that there would not be in future. And that *"regular access to a child underpins prevention"*. Thus not only does monitoring discover abuse according to North Lincolnshire LEA, but it also prevents it from happening. This begs the question of why so much abuse occurs within families whose children are attending school regularly or already known to social services. Sight of a child for an hour every six months does not prevents abuse any more than regular school attendance does and to subject every home educator's human rights to routine disregard will not alter this situation.

One LEA seemed to be of the opinion that the guidance could actually change the legal situation (which of course it does not, the guidance is just that and has no status in law). The East Riding of Yorkshire LEA said:

"I am pleased that you have strengthened the guidance with respect to Child Protection and a better right of access to see the child where there are real concerns about a child's welfare."

The idea that someone should have the right to see a child where there are real concerns is not of course the issue, though what constitutes a 'real concern' may be more of an issue as can be seen from what The East Riding of Yorkshire LEA went on to say:

"We have had instances where we have not known if a child was dead or alive because of parental refusal to allow access over a considerable period of time."

The second statement begs the question of the first statement of just what is a 'real concern'. It seems likely that a real concern in their minds is equated by the child not being seen by their officer, though in fact the child is likely being seen by family, neighbours, doctors, perhaps community leaders, swimming pool attendants and a whole range of other adults in the community. What this LEA is effectively saying is that having no evidence that the child is at risk is enough to raise a concern even though the law would require a positive reason for concern that a child is at significant harm.

The submission by Southampton LEA fell into the category of being a plea for change rather than a response to the guidance on existing law. They raised the issue of the 'Every Child Matters' policy, which is not legislation, but itself a guidance document which has no status in law. They objected that the DfES guidance on home education does not take the every child matters policy into account. Perhaps another way of looking at this might be to acknowledge that the Every Child Matters Policy fails to take into account actual legislative powers and duties and does not, therefore, provide a workable policy, but more a wish list of powers that LEAs would prefer to be true.

Another example of confusion over the purpose of the guidance comes from Cambridgeshire's submission, many parts of which seem to be suggesting that the DfES guidance should not be issuing guidance to law as it is, but should rather be giving guidance which supports LEAs in going beyond what is legally permissible. A clear example of this is the statement *"The statement in the guidance that parents are not legally required to notify the LEA should they decide to home educate is a further concern to this Authority (8.4 and 3.9). This Authority believes that an opportunity exists to close what is in effect a loophole but that the guidance has not addressed this"*.

Leeds said that they know of 150 home educating parents in their area and are able to do home visits with around 98% of families partly because the home educators *"are not aware that they need not agree to meet us!"* This is a clear admission that Leeds LEA has no intention of informing parents of their rights. Their submission went on to say that *Education Otherwise's* support for parent's human rights by supporting families who do not permit home visits was to be regarded as, *"exploitation of the situation"*. Leeds also suggested the improbable scenario where it might be possible for the DfES to negotiate a protocol with EO in order to recruit this major home education support organisation to their way of thinking so that EO would allow or encourage home visits to its members.

The submission from Bedford LEA stated that *"access is needed"*. They also were concerned about the DfES' use of the phrase 'reasonable cause' in relation to welfare concerns as *"it is not explained"*. Clearly Bedford LEA are unclear as to what constitutes 'reasonable cause for concern' which, given the amount of welfare training currently in place for anyone working with children, is extremely worrying.

Cambridgeshire once again come at the issue of 'concern' most bluntly. In response to paragraph 3.19 *"the authority must have demonstrable grounds for concern and must outline those grounds to the parent when requesting access to their home"* Cambridgeshire state, *"This Authority believes that this particular piece of guidance is unhelpful".*

It is Havering LEA that raises the spectre of the Victoria Climbié case. They begin their response with the statement that *"Victoria Climbié was not on a school roll",* and outrageously attempting to link Victoria's death with home education to justify home visits and the introduction of monitoring procedures, despite the fact that Victoria was visited and was already the subject of social services enquiries. Victoria was in fact not in school because her LEA did not have any school place available within the authority. She was not electively home educated, but came under the auspices of the LEA's EOTAS (Education Otherwise than at School) services and so visits should have been built into this provision. Her family allowed both the social services and the local education authority access to both her and the home. She was already on the 'At Risk Register' and had an allocated social worker when she was tragically murdered.

The failures which led to Victoria's death were not in any way related to a lack of powers to see her or gain access to her home but rather a failure on the part of statutory authorities to use existing powers to protect a child for whom they already had significant evidence of being at serious risk of harm. A change in home education legislation would not have saved her. It is difficult to see the raising of the Victoria Climbié case as being anything other than a desperate attempt to justify the unjustifiable. It is somewhat cynical as well as ill informed to attempt to gain powers to breach the human rights of all home educating families by using an unrelated and shocking case to engage people's emotional response in the absence of any rational argument.

ii. De-registrations

De-registration for the purposes of home educating a child are governed by the Pupil Registration Regulations 2005 section 9 (1)(c), These are under review and we can expect to see new regulations published either in 2006 or 2007. Currently schools must deregister a child on demand in England and Wales unless the child is registered at a special school. The proprietor of the school must inform the LEA within ten working days that this has happened. There is some doubt among legal experts about the process where a school attendance order is in force; it may or may not be possible to de-register a child with an existing order.

From the consultation responses it appears that several LEAs do not understood the regulations. In their response Surrey LEA, for example, claim that the LEA should *"be satisfied that appropriate arrangements have been made **prior** to a school place being de-registered or at time of transfer"* (*their emphasis*).

This kind of misunderstanding is not uncommon. Nottingham LEA has guidance on their website telling Head Teachers to *"keep the child on roll for a maximum of 15 school days and mark their attendance as 'not required on site' "*. This is quite simply illegal. North Lincolnshire goes further in wanting *"a 'period of notice' which would allow all parties to prepare appropriately"*.

iii. Compulsory registration of home educators

Leeds LEA also raised the issue of changing legislation by suggesting that home educators should be forced to register with their LEA on the grounds of 'educational and Health and Safety'. The North East London cluster added that they wanted parents to be forced to register with their LEA. Surrey wanted the guidance to be altered to say that parents had a compulsory obligation to register with the LEA even though that is not the legal situation and no such obligation exists.

iv. Educational assessment.

As has previously been stated the legal remit of LEAs in regard to home educators is narrow and framed in the negative. Despite this LEAs persist in inflating their duties to assess education according to criteria of their own choosing. Not only is there no basis for this in English law, but the second sentence of Protocol 2 Article 1 of the European Convention of Human Rights says:

> *"In the exercise of any functions which it assumes in relation to education and to teaching, the State shall respect the right of parents to ensure such education and teaching in conformity with their own religious and philosophical convictions."*

Here 'philosophical convictions' includes any parental convictions relating to education. This was itself part of a decision made by the European courts:

> *"The second sentence of Article 2 (P1-A2) implies ... The State is forbidden to pursue an aim of indoctrination that might be considered as not respecting parents' religious and philosophical convictions. That is the limit that must not be exceeded."*

But what is meant by philosophical and can this extend to pedagogy? In another ruling relating to the use of corporal punishment in a Scottish school prior to it being outlawed in the UK the European courts ruled that 'convictions':

> *"is more akin to the term 'beliefs' (in the French text: 'convictions') appearing in Article 9 (art. 9) - which guarantees freedom of thought, conscience and religion - and denotes views that attain a certain level of cogency, seriousness, cohesion and importance."*

From this context it emerges that 'philosophical convictions' means any serious, cohesive belief held to be important by parents must be taken as the primary measure by which education is determined as efficient. It is the parents who have the legal right to define the criteria against which their education can be seen as efficient and suitable.

LEAs frequently fail to take this on board. North Yorkshire LEA considers that parents are required to *"demonstrate that their child is making reasonable progress"*, but there is no such legal requirement. The Cluster group of North East London LEAs thought that LEAs believes that they should *"fulfil their responsibilities and assume nothing"* which simply misunderstands the nature of their duties and responsibilities.

Calderdale takes the first sentence of Article 1 Protocol 2 of the European Convention on Human Rights, i.e. *"No person shall be denied the right to education"* and interprets it to mean that local authorities should be able to set the standards of achievement for home educated children. They have clearly not read the second sentence of Protocol 2, or find it inconvenient to do so.

One or two LEAs seem to think that it is their role to determine whether the educational choices of the parents are also those of the child's. Havering for example says *"If the child is not seen it is impossible to verify that home education is also the child's choice"*. In law it simply is not the child's choice, it is the parents. Surrey LEA go so far as to request a statutory obligation be placed on children to *"attend any meetings that may be arranged to express his/her views in some way or other"*.

Clearly these concerns for children's rights are completely disingenuous and betray an underlying hostility towards home education. The authors of these suggestions fail to see the irony that when children 'chooses' not to attend school while enrolled by truanting, then their parents can be jailed for an offence under Section 444 of the 1996 Education Act. When children do not want to go to school Educational Welfare services do not insist that the child's views be respected and that the parents must home educate in accordance with the child's wishes. Nor of course is every child in school routinely asked if he or she would rather not attend school and be home educated.

Other LEAs fail to understand the nature of their basic duty with respect to home education issues. Doncaster LEA shows this most clearly:

> *"There is a duty placed upon the LEAs to be satisfied that education is satisfactory it cannot just assume that the child is receiving an education and take no action to address its legal duty."*

In fact there is no such duty in law. LEAs only need to ask for evidence if they have an actual reason to think no education is taking place. Southampton also believes that they have a duty not only to assess the education, but to monitor it. Once again no such duty exists, Southampton talk about determining whether the education is 'efficient and suitable' without paying any attention to the first limb of Section 437 of the 1996 Education Act which first requires them to have a reason for supposing no education is taking place. Leeds complain that 'evidence' provided by parents fails to show how children are progressing, but fail to appreciate that they should not be initially asking for evidence and that 'progress' as defined by the LEA, is not a criteria that parents have any obligation to accept. They also complain to the DfES that parents often turn to solicitors to make complaints about LEA harassment after they insist on being given *"information we regard as reasonable"*. This again misses the point that in law it is the parents who have the right to choose what information to offer in order to satisfy the LEA. It is not for the LEA to 'insist' on any particular type or style of information or evidence.

The Head of Welfare Education Services for Cambridge LEA seems to be of the opinion that in stating that there is ambiguity in the law. In response to the DfES assertion that, *"LEAs can intervene should they have reason to believe that parents are not providing a suitable education"*. Cambridge LEA objects that:

"[the guidance] seems to imply that the LEA requires clear and demonstrable grounds in order to intervene - i.e. the LEA needs to have specific evidence to justify an enquiry... Clearly then, by implication, some parents will not be required to demonstrate that suitable home education is being provided. This is a very grey area and the draft guidance appears to be open to misinterpretation".

Cambridge LEA are right to conclude that some (probably most) parents will not be required to demonstrate that suitable home education is being provided; they only have to do so if there are grounds for supposing no education is taking place. However, there is no grey area here. The LEA is simply refusing to believe that the law is as it is. Cambridge are attempting to insist that the DfES has misinterpreted the law in saying that an LEA has no duty to make enquiries unless they have reason to believe that there is no education taking place, as it stated in Section 437 of the 1996 Education act. This is not a mudded interpretation of a grey area by the DfES, it is simply a legal fact.

Many LEAs (for example the South West regional group of LEAs) argued for one part of the guidance to be deleted. The section that offended them came in paragraph 3.17 of the guidance where the DfES list possible, but not exhaustive, alternatives to home visits. One such option is *to "have the educational provision endorsed by a recognised third party."* This is a method used by many home educators to provide information or evidence. It might be used because the relationship between the family and the LEA has broken down or where the family do not feel the LEA would give them a fair hearing, or might be likely not to understand their method of education, particularly where the family follow an autonomous, child-led educational approach. It might simply be that the family value a particular level of privacy or that such a report enables them to retain control of their own evidence. In these cases families will make use of a sympathetic, qualified teacher, educational psychologist or other education expert, sometimes known to the family or contacted through support networks within the home education community. The expert can make an independent assessment of the provision and write a report to the LEA, with their professional status guaranteeing the credibility of the report.

It can only be guessed why so many LEAs object to the use of independent experts. If their concern is for the educational welfare of the children then it is hard to imagine why such a method should present any problems. If on the other hand their main concern is their own exercise of intrusive power or they are simply hostile to the whole philosophy of home education then it might be easier to understand why they object to qualified experts favourably assessing home education provision.

Doncaster believes that home educator's routinely lie in their responses to enquiries. They wrote *"it is not good enough to accept a written report or bibliography as evidence of education taking place. A written report does not mean that what is reported is taking place"*. Yet. if an LEA issues an SAO and subsequently takes the family to court for not registering the child at school, the court will certainly not call the child to give evidence (indeed the magistrate would take a dim view of an attempt by either the parent or an LEA to bring a young child into a judicial setting on such flimsy grounds). Nor would the court expect to see the home but would accept the very same documents that Doncaster call 'lies' as adequate evidence, providing of course that there was no other evidence to suggest that the parent was perjuring himself in court. It seems perverse, not to mention a waste of public funds, for the LEA to refuse to accept evidence which a court will readily find acceptable.

Two particularly extreme views were expressed by Surrey and North Lincolnshire LEAs. North Lincolnshire wanted to have the power to expect 'Standardised Evidencing' which, while not clarified as to what they meant looked very much like a call for standardised testing. This completely cuts across the parental human right to decide on the nature of their child's education. Surrey LEA suggested that OFSTED should be involved in the process by having access to samples of home educated children's work, again making assumptions about what kind of evidence is acceptable without any legal right to do so.

v. SEN statements

Several LEAs misunderstand the powers of a Statement of Special Educational Needs. The DfES guidance says clearly that a Statement of Special Educational Needs should normally be maintained when a family are home educating, however an SEN statement only refers to that provision which an LEA should provide were the child registered at a maintained school, or otherwise unable to attend such a school through illness. In other words the parents of a home educated child cannot be made to provide what the statement says the LEA should provide (the provision as laid out in section 3 and 4 of a statement). Additionally, where a statement is maintained (for whatever purpose) the LEA must review the statement annually. However, this review process does not legally require that the child be present for any part of the review.

Cambridgeshire LEA believe that *"access to the child is crucial"* and that *"a personal adviser is required to attend the year 9 review, contribute to and oversee the delivery of the transition plan"* clearly assuming that there can be a plan which has a role to play in home education. While some home educating parents find statements useful in obtaining other services which the child may still be entitled to, many other home educating parents do not see any purpose to a statement. A statement cannot force the LEA to make any provision as the child is home educated, nor can it force the parents to make the provision it identifies.

vi. Reviewing internal LEA policies

A growing number of LEAs have adopted a positive approach to reviewing their internal policies with regard to home education. Most notably, Milton Keynes has done so in consultation with local home educators and has arrived at a mutually acceptable policy. Other regions of the UK have also successfully undertaken such consultations. The Scottish Executive held extensive meetings with home educators over a period of years before issuing their guidance, which ultimately, following much detailed debate, were accepted by all parties. Similarly OFSTED include in their guidance to inspection teams that LEAs should undertake consultations with home educators in drawing up their policies.

However, there are LEAs which are clearly threatened by and resistant to the notion of including the client group in any form of consultation. Cambridgeshire do not consider consultation to be good practice:

> *"Whilst always welcoming discussion with and the involvement of other stakeholders this Authority is doubtful as to the appropriateness of formally involving Education Otherwise and similar organisations and home educating parents in the review of its internal policies and practices."*

The understated level of contempt for the home education community in this statement is more worthy of 'Sir Humphrey Appleton' than of a modern example of transparent decision making and democracy. The Head of Cambridge's Education Welfare Services gives no reason for singling out the home education community for such draconian exclusion.

vi. Flexi-schooling

This was an interesting issue. Some LEAs consider flexi-schooling to be an illegal practice, but one LEA, the East Riding of Yorkshire, stated:

"The view of this LEA is that flexi-education is a good thing and that it begins to pave the road to the future of education for all children – the road to fully personalised and individualised learning".

Surrey LEA, however, was simply confused over the issue, wrongly believing that special funding would be necessary to allow flexi-schooling.

viii. Costs

LEAs do not receive any direct funding to cover the costs of home education and several LEAs raised this as an issue, particularly in relation to the rising cost of monitoring home education. Some LEAs appear to perform this work with no allocated budget of any kind, fitting the work in around other duties. Many LEAs still have no designated worker with any experience or training on the subject. Since the home education community is growing this problem will continue to worsen unless it is addressed by government.

LEAs were particularly concerned at the call by the DfES for them to consider providing other services to home educators such as police checks, assisting with the arrangement of work placements and providing parents with lists of available tutors from their home tuition service lists. All of these have cost implications and a number of LEAs said, quite reasonably, that these costs would need to be covered before they would feel able to offer such services.

Conclusions

The first and main conclusion to be drawn about both the DfES staff involved in drawing up policy and guidance regarding home education and the LEA staff who implement this policy is that they are surprisingly poorly informed about the duties and powers under which they work. LEAs urgently need to address the training they make available to staff.

These response documents make clear that LEAs are obsessed by the concern that they do not have the powers they believe they need to fulfil the duties they understand they have. In fact the reason that they do not have the powers they seem to so urgently want is that neither do they have the duties they imagine.

LEAs overall do not appear to appreciate the fact that in law, whether they are dealing with human rights legislation or education law, the duty to provide for a child's educational and welfare needs primarily rests with the parents, not with the State. The State only has a role to act in cases where there are actual grounds for believing that there is a serious cause for concern, namely significant risk of harm. It is not for the State to proactively seek to determine that this is so with no evidence to the contrary, nor to decide that all home educating parents are liars. It is impossible to come to any conclusion in reading these submissions other than that the underlying attitude of most of the LEAs replying to the DfES consultation is that parents are simply not to be trusted to look after their own children. They appear to argue for a State in which a priori, every child should be considered to be at risk unless regularly seen by themselves. The fact that so many LEAs wanted the right to refuse to accept third party reports of educational provision betrays an even deeper mistrust; LEAs not only want to assume that parents are liars, but also that independent experts who may not share their mistrust are also to be treated with suspicion.

It is of urgent concern that many LEAs see any parent who chooses to home educate as a threat to the welfare of her own children. It is deeply worrying that a vociferous group of LEAs want powers to set the criteria for education without regard to the culture or philosophy of individual families and in the face of human rights legislation. Katerina Tomasevski, the Special Rapporteur to the United Nations Commission on Human Rights has said that:

> "The respect of parent's freedom to educate their children according to their vision of what education should be has been part of international human rights standards since their very emergence."

If those policies desired by the officials represented in this consultation were to be adopted then the primacy of the family and the right of parents to educate and parent their own children would be lost forever; education and parenting styles would become the subjects only of State policy.

Chapter four:

But What About University?

"What right have your children to go to university after they opted out of school?" I was recently asked.

It was both a disturbing and a revealing question, particularly coming from someone who was employed by the government with a remit for home education. There is an opinion that clearly thinks that if children do not play the game of sacrificing their childhoods to eleven years of school learning, plus another two years of A level studies then they cannot be allowed entrance to a higher education system which, when it is working at its best, is much more similar to home education than to school.

Good university education requires self motivation, research skills, time management, strategies for learner managed learning. These are all things that home educators tend to stress either explicitly, or simply by the nature of having children who play significant roles in managing their own education from young ages.

In the States increasing numbers of universities set aside places for home educated children, recognising that the experience of years of intrinsically motivated learning is likely to stand these children in good stead to thrive at university level, whether or not they have standard paper qualifications. So in 1997 Meighan noted a letter from the Boston University Undergraduates Admissions Director,

> *"Boston University welcomes applications from home schooled students. We believe students educated primarily at home possess the passion for knowledge, the independence and self reliance that enable them to excel in our intellectually challenging programs of study."* (Meighan, 1997)

This is backed up by Grace Llewellyn's findings after interviewing twenty-seven admission directors. Although three were sceptical of home educator's abilities, none of the directors said they would refuse to consider candidates on merit in the context of their particular educational experiences, rather than requiring standard qualifications. Colleges that had previously enrolled home-schoolers were particularly enthusiastic.

The news of a rising number of young people who have charted their own educational courses and have much to offer and gain at degree level is slower to filter into British universities, but there is increasing evidence that young people with alternative backgrounds can access higher education. In a research dissertation for her degree Travena Whitbread contacted thirty colleges and universities and found only three who maintained that they would require specific qualifications about which they were not prepared to be flexible. In all other cases, university admissions departments said that they would consider candidates on an individual basis, much as they would for mature applicants, and would want to meet the young person to discuss their achievements before taking a decision.

It seems that there is at least a climate of open-mindedness, but when it comes to actually getting a place at university there is a vast breadth of opinion and procedure. In Issue 154 of the *Education Otherwise* newsletter there is an account of a young man who gained access straight on to a master's degree in physics (MPhys). He did three GCSEs from home, gaining B grades in chemistry and physics, but only a D in maths. Despite this he went on to do a maths A level, along with physics and environmental science. J was dyslexic, did not have the 'required' GCSEs to be allowed to do his three preferred A levels at sixth form and did not have any qualification in English, yet at his interview a Professor of Theoretical Physics declared that he would do 'anything legally possible' to make sure J got onto the degree course on the strength of the way he was able to talk about his subject with a passionate professional.

Another home educated student has recently been offered a place to study a degree in 3D Graphic Design and IT. On the strength of the portfolio he had developed at home, using sophisticated software and developing digital art as a self taught student, this candidate was given an unconditional offer to Bournemouth University without GCSEs or A levels and despite a specific learning problem of dyslexia. The portfolio was considered so innovative and of such a high standard that it outweighed any other criteria.

From Prejudice to Misunderstanding

At the other end of the scale there are still institutions, or perhaps more accurately individuals making decisions on behalf of institutions, determined to only operate within the most narrow-minded of tick box determined to only operate within the most narrow-minded of tick box systems. One applicant who had done undergraduate level study at the Open University amounting to 180 points (half a degree) enquired of Sheffield Hallam University whether her educational background and achievements would be accepted for a particular BSc course. On the strength of this L. was warmly invited to apply, at which point the course staff decided that they could not judge whether Open University qualifications were good enough to accept as equivalents to GCSEs and rejected the application.

When pressed the staff said that they were most concerned about the applicant's qualification in English and would get in touch with the OU in order to reconsider. (The applicant had completed a ten point level one course in English). They then took almost two months to come up with the final response that, *"Academic members of staff have now looked at the content of the Level One Maths for Science unit and they confirm that it is of an equivalent academic level to GCSE Maths".* They went on to say that they none the less would not accept it. They completely ignored the fact that the candidate had also done a much more extensive science foundation course that included significant amounts of Maths, including Maths to support physics of approximately A level standard. Just as surprising was the fact that they had originally told the candidate that they were concerned about her English qualification, not the maths one.

The only conclusion that can be drawn is that the staff of this particular department were extremely cavalier in inviting an application without paying attention to the information they had been given. They then made a decision based on not wanting to take the time to look at anything that did not fit the standard mould, even when that something was more than they would usually be offered.

Home educators do not have a 'route' to go through when making initial enquiries. On the one hand they are more like mature candidates who might be bringing alternative backgrounds to bear on university entry, but on the other hand they often apply at the standard age of eighteen or nineteen so they do not fit easily into the mature applicant's profile. Many academics are able to approach these applicants with sympathy, but others are systematically unwilling to think about a candidate who requires some measure of individual engagement. In the absence of any systematic thinking about how university admissions tutors might approach home educated young people, this means that decisions rest on individual initiative or prejudice and even within one university two departments may make vastly different responses.

One home educated young person recently applied to medical schools. Birmingham University replied that they would only accept the standard set of GCSEs and A levels (the candidate was offering 240 points of OU degree level study including a full 60 point course in second year chemistry; 360 points being a full degree). When this approach was questioned Professor Christopher Lote, Associate Dean of the medical school at Birmingham University repeated that no equivalents to GCSE English and Maths would be considered and that, *"We... are not easily convinced that some qualifications ARE higher than A levels"*. It appears that Professor Lote doubts that OU courses at undergraduate level are even on a par with A levels.

The same young person was told by Cardiff University that if she wanted to study medicine she would be best advised to take a full degree course before applying (advice that would have disqualified her from having her tuition fees met by the NHS bursary and hardly a reasonable demand as an equivalent to A levels). He added that if she applied the university would, *"require a statement from the LEA advisor which has had responsibility for monitoring your home education"*. As no such person exists this would be more than difficult to satisfy.

Another young person with similar OU qualifications was told he would not be considered to study Genetics at Manchester University, whilst Roehampton University wrote to a home educated enquirer that *"even home educated students..."* must have the standard GCSE and A level package and nothing else could be considered. The response of Neil Murray, the admissions officer for Bath Spa University to a home educated candidate with two A levels plus a 60 point OU foundation course was that, *"Our academic staff might need to be persuaded that you would benefit from conventional teaching methods"*.

One university admissions tutor in archaeology told us that the reluctance of some departments to look at non-standard backgrounds comes down to an increasing defensiveness. With league tables now becoming a feature of higher education and with increasing pressure to turn out highly standardised graduates, he felt that many admissions tutors would become increasingly wary of taking a risk by accepting any kind of 'different' candidate. He did say that personally he would be willing to look at a home educated applicant with no formal qualifications if the person had practical experience of archaeology and was articulate about the subject, but he stressed that he thought himself unusual in this approach and that he would feel vulnerable in making such a decision.

All of this makes dismal reading and it is a sad reflection that our allegedly highest institutes of learning can be so lacking in imagination or simply so intellectually lazy and/or dismissive. Despite this, the overall picture is far from negative.

Finding Flexibility in University Admissions

In medicine, one of the most difficult subjects for any young person to gain entry into, we found that attitudes were more often flexible and innovative than not. Liverpool University had a sticking point over the issue of English and Maths GCSEs (even where there were other qualifications in place that went beyond Maths GCSE), but was otherwise helpful and had even produced a policy document outlining which OU courses they would accept in lieu of A levels. Plymouth Medical School was not only happy to look at equivalents, but had actually gone so far as to develop a policy for non-standard entrants, asking them to sit the GAMSAT, a medical aptitude entrance exam. The admissions officer at Hull and York Medical School cheerfully engaged in detailed research liaising with the Open University to advise a candidate on what would be the best courses to take to gain entry. Other universities were actively welcoming of a non standard candidate and stressed their willingness to look at the individual, including Cambridge which was happy to waive matriculation requirements. Several other medical schools expressed flexible and welcoming attitudes and Oxford acknowledged that whilst this was *"uncharted territory"* they were none the less willing to look at individual cases.

Our research focused on four other degree areas: a BSc in Genetics, a BSc in Nursing (including the professional registered nurse certification) and B.A. degrees in literature/creative writing and politics/social science. In all of these areas the negative responses were by far the minority.

In Genetics, Aberystwyth invited a home educated young person for an informal chat and were happy to make an offer following this. Wolverhampton, the University of the West of England and Nottingham were also positive.

In nursing the NHS careers website explicitly says that as a guideline each 30 point OU course should be accepted as an A level equivalent and each 60 point course as two A levels. It also states that although two A levels are the norm for entry into degree level nursing there is no absolute requirement. The applicant in question had a 60 point mixed science course and two 30 point courses, plus a further five 10 point courses including Maths, English and three specialist science modules. Hull and Oxford Brookes showed particular openness and the University of Central England Birmingham was especially helpful and interested, meeting the student and going on to make an unconditional offer.

In terms of departments offering B.A. degrees several universities in this study expressed keen interest in interviewing and/or making an offer to a student who came with something 'different' than the standard school background. Oxford Brookes' admissions officer wrote, *"I would encourage you to put in an application through UCAS, and not to be deterred by the fact that your entry route is not a typical one"*. Aberystwyth was again particularly positive, writing, *"We have a very flexible admissions policy"*. Similarly, Gloucestershire, Newport, Lancashire, York, Sheffield Hallam, Bangor, Bristol, Lincoln and Lancaster all showed considerable interest and flexibility.

It is perhaps particularly interesting that Sheffield Hallam's English department showed such flexibility given the rather intransigent attitude of staff in the nursing department. The message seems to be that higher education opportunities for young people with non-standard backgrounds do exist, but finding them might require making detailed and early informal enquiries to sift the attitudes of individual staff. No university that we approached had any coherent overall policy towards home educators across departmental boundaries, although Aberystwyth consistent showed the most flexibility across departments.

Sample of university responses to home educated candidates across sample subject areas:

University/department	Inflexible attitude – will only look at standard qualifications	Some flexibility – will consider equivalents at A level, but insists on maths & English GCSEs	Flexible – willing to consider the individual on merit or has a selection mechanism in place
MEDICINE:			
Birmingham	X		
Hull & York			X
Bristol			X
Cambridge			X
Plymouth			X
Liverpool		X	
Cardiff	X		
Leicester			X
St. George – London			X .
Oxford			X
Southampton	X		
Sheffield			X
Newcastle			X
GENETICS:			
Nottingham			X
Aberystwyth			X
Sheffield			X
Wolverhampton			X
University of the West of England			X
Manchester	X		
NURSING:			
University of Central England			X
Oxford Brooks			X
Hull			X
Sheffield Hallam		X	
ENGLISH &/or SOCIAL SCIENCE			
University of Central Lancashire			X
Oxford Brookes			X
Gloucestershire			X
Roehampton	X		
Aberystwyth			X
Newport			X
Bath Spa	X		
York			X
Sheffield Hallam			X
Bangor			X
Bristol			X
Lincoln			X
Lancaster			X
Cambridge			X
Newcastle			X

The Open University: providing alternative pathways

In the sample of young people applying for university courses, the routes taken included studying A levels via distance learning providers and/or accessing Open University courses as A level equivalents. None of these young people had undertaken GCSEs and in all but a minority of cases this was not an issue for the universities consulted.

Another issue that arose from this was that the OU was seen as providing a range of educational pathways. Individual OU courses were taken in lieu of A levels and the young people using these courses unanimously felt that the courses were more interesting and better presented than A levels they had studied. One young person had abandoned a Biology A level (being taken via the National Extension College) part way through the second year because she was consistently getting assignment scores of 100% and felt that the course lacked any challenge. She switched to a 60 point OU science foundation course (S103). Another student had successfully completed a Philosophy A level and was half way through an English A level before deciding to switch to an OU 60 point humanities foundation course which covered not only English Literature and some Philosophy, but also an introduction to the History of Music, History of Art and Architecture and History.

The Open University's graduated courses provide a range of differentiated learning in a wide number of disciplines. Several young people have found 10 point courses (perhaps roughly equivalent to GCSE in level of study, but shorter in duration) to be a good bridge between informal and structured learning styles, with the added benefit that short OU courses are often more interesting and better focused than GCSEs (whether the topic is the human genome or a study of the life and thinking of Leonardo Da Vinci). It is also beneficial that such courses are cheaper to study than individual GCSEs when taken with support from a distance learning college, as well taking only ten to twenty weeks to complete. For all of these reasons OU courses can provide excellent routes into a style of structured learning that suits flexible home education lifestyles.

decided instead to continue with an OU degree. The reasons for this were several and included that she felt the structure of the degree and style of self motivated learning better suited her previous experience of home education, and that an OU degree was more affordable and would not result in large debts. Since the student was already using OU courses as A level equivalents she was also able to 'begin' her degree having already half completed the first year. Another home educator who opted for OU study had disability needs that she felt were more easily addressed by living at home and studying part time. In short, the OU can effectively act as both an access route to taking a traditional degree or as a degree provider in its own right with easy conversion between the two possibilities.

For some home educators this has led to an interest in using OU courses at younger ages. The Open University student newsletter, *Sesame*, recently carried an article about online facilities for 'school-aged' students. It is an article that reveals some assumptions that home educators are beginning to challenge. Anyone who has ever tried to register a young person under eighteen for an OU course you will know that online registration is not possible; the date of birth triggers automatic rejection. Families that persist are almost invariably told that registering an under 18, or even an under 16, year old student is not possible. Best guess is that many families desist at this stage, and yet the barriers are not so obvious for school students if the figures given by the assistant secretary of the OU's student services, Steve Clayton, are anything to go by.

> *"There are just over 2,000 students on the Young Applicants in Schools Scheme. These students are supported by their schools and the university to study an OU course alongside their AS/A level studies."* (Sesame, Spring 2006)

If a student is 'in the system' then the OU is potentially open. Pupils already studying three or four 'A' levels can be faced with adding a quarter or even a half work-load of a first year undergraduate to their timetable with added pressure to perform on the recommendation of schools and financed by local education authorities. Conversely, when a home educated young person applies to join the OU the story can be rather different. Fears that the student would not 'cope', even though she may be doing only OU work without the added burden of GCSEs or A levels, may be expressed. The logic is that when a teacher recommends a child for a course, the teacher is an expert whose judgement can be trusted, whereas a parent requesting such access is more likely to be treated as an amateur over-estimating the capabilities of his offspring.

local education authorities. Conversely, when a home educated young person applies to join the OU the story can be rather different. Fears that the student would not 'cope', even though she may be doing only OU work without the added burden of GCSEs or A levels, may be expressed. The logic is that when a teacher recommends a child for a course, the teacher is an expert whose judgement can be trusted, whereas a parent requesting such access is more likely to be treated as an amateur over-estimating the capabilities of his offspring.

One family in our research was first told that registering a fifteen-year-old for a course could not be done, that it was never done. When they persisted they were asked to verify that the young person could benefit from the course by getting permission from their LEA. From a purely practical point of view, no LEA is likely to have detailed knowledge of an individual home educated child's capabilities, interests and learning needs. More fundamentally, it is home education parents, not LEAs, who are legally responsible for the philosophy and content of their child's education. Finally, it was decided that the decision would be based on the young person's own application, in conjunction with the parents' assessment of her ability to do the course, the consent of the OU academic staff concerned and the final ratification of the Regional Director. This took over three months, and the involvement of different tiers of administrative and academic staff caused some confusion along the way. At one stage an email from an academic staff member gave permission to register the young person, but was followed by a letter from an administrator saying there were two more stages to go through before a decision would be made. What was clear was that home educators were seen as odd and that, unlike school sponsored OU students, no process had been imagined for dealing with home educators. This is backed up by Steve Clayton's aside that,

> "There is also a very small number of individual students studying at home under special arrangements." (Sesame, Spring 2006)

In other words every home educating family who approaches the OU is expected to re-invent the wheel in order to register. Since the OU has a regional structure the attitude to home educators varies enormously. The Welsh region has been particularly approachable and flexible, using informal telephone interviews with parents and children as well as written statements about what the young person is hoping to gain from the course as guidelines to register young people, both under 18s and under 16s. In Wales there are has been a young person aged 15 enrolled to study a 60 point science course (half a full undergraduate timetable), another beginning a 30 point language course just before his 15th birthday, and 15 and 16-year-old young people studying 10 and 30 point courses in Sciences, Maths and Computing.

The Oxford region is similarly flexible and has appointed someone to oversee applications from younger students. The London region, on the other hand, has shown flexibility towards young people between the age of 16 and 18, setting up an interview system, but seems intransigent when it comes to under 16s. One family have been told that a child under 16 must have A levels before she is allowed to do an OU course (though once she is 16 there will be no need for her to possess any qualification)

As with mainstream universities this patchwork approach to admission has drawbacks. Families have to show a lot of perseverance and tact, and even then may sometimes face uncompromising officials with no intention of looking at individual cases. On the other hand, the lack of hard and fast lines gives home educators an almost unique freedom to argue every case on its merit. If either mainstream universities or the Open University were to introduce criteria for entry there is the danger that these could become inflexible or draw the kind of boundaries that home education by its nature seeks to blur if not eradicate. The present lack of a system is clumsy, but it does allow for a great deal of flexibility.

Another degree route related to the OU exists through the Open College of Art. The college offers distance learning courses in a range of subjects from drawing and painting to sculpture and textiles, from photography to creative writing. The courses are modular, can be studied either as one off units without formal assessment or assessed for degree points under the auspices of the University of Glamorgan. The degree points can also be used as part of Open University degrees for those who want to build bespoke degrees including both practical arts and academic disciplines. Like OU courses the points from units can also be used to gain qualifications in lieu of A levels and one of the young people in our study was using a mixture of OU and OCA courses in this way.

The person asking what right home educators have to go to university may have been perturbed by the fact that home educators routinely expose the fallacy that in order to get a 'good education' children have to be drilled and coerced for eleven or thirteen years of their childhoods. In this study young people going on to higher education, both mainstream and OU degrees, had unfailingly spent their so called 'school years' pursuing their own interests with complete flexibility. They did not come from families that followed any curricula or timetables. Much of their learning was completely informal and revolved around visits, play and conversation.

It is perhaps not surprising that the OU featured as a good route for both A level equivalents and degrees. After all it is an institution that has fundamentally questioned the commonly held belief that undergraduates should come from backgrounds of formal academic success with a clutch of A levels and GCSEs. In its early days the OU had to struggle for credibility, but today it is ranked highly alongside many mainstream universities even though it continues to routinely take in people who have not 'succeeded' at school. The OU, like many home educators, explodes the myth of needing GCSEs and A levels before a student can benefit from a degree, and ultimately that is the only indicator of a 'right' to a university education – that the person in question will benefit from it and, in so doing, will bring benefits to others.

Conclusions

1. In the past there has been a steady stream of anecdotal evidence of home educated young people accessing higher education with no formal qualifications, using completely alternative routes such as a portfolio of art or written work or evidence of long-term work experience (e.g. work in a theatre being used to go on to study drama). There are still instances of this highly flexible approach, such as the young person recently made an unconditional offer to study design and IT at Bournemouth University. This is a particularly appropriate route for home educated young people who may not have studied any formal exam subjects, but who often develop extremely well informed and passionate interests in particular fields, sometimes going well beyond what would be expected within more narrowly defined curricula at GCSE or even A level.

2. The pressures of league tables and an increasingly standardised approach to education are factors that militate against home educated young people who may seek access to higher education from non standard backgrounds.

3. Increasing numbers of home educators do appear to be entering children for GCSEs and A levels. However, this can present significant logistical difficulties. Children in a home environment are not likely to cram for eight to ten GCSEs at a time and in any case the cost of this could be prohibitive for many home educating families, who tend to be of lower than average income. GCSEs have the added problem of requiring external marking for course work, and although using distance learning centres may be a

solution, it can be a relatively expensive one. Finding exam centres for external candidates can be extremely hard in some areas and again can add to the expense, with some centres charging only their costs while others see home educators as a way to make significant profits.

4. It appears that many home educators go into mainstream further education colleges at sixteen in order to complete GCSEs and/or A levels and so gain a conventional background to add to their earlier home education background before going on to university.

5. The Open University (and associated colleges such as the Open College of Art) provides an excellent route into formal learning for home educated young people, delivering courses that can be used either in lieu of GCSEs and A levels or as the foundation for building degrees studied at home.

6. The evidence of the Open University is that people without formal academic backgrounds can do extremely well at degree level. Although the numbers are currently small there is also evidence of home educated young people thriving on OU courses from ages as young as 14, even when they have done no structured work before this point. It therefore seems reasonable to call for a flexible approach from universities. There are many ways to demonstrate that someone is capable of benefiting from a particular degree and not to take this on board wastes potential and contributes to social exclusion.

7. It is refreshing to see that many university departments are willing to take a flexible view of non standard backgrounds. The rule of thumb of accepting 10 point OU courses as GCSE equivalents and 30 point courses as A level equivalents with 60 point courses fulfilling two A levels was one that many departments in this study were willing to adopt as a guideline. However, there is still a gap when it comes to those whose backgrounds do not include any or 'enough' paper qualifications. There needs to be pressure from the home education community in dialogue with university admissions tutors to widen access for young people presenting relevant portfolios or those with an articulate oral knowledge of a subject area. (Research has previously shown that conversation is the major learning tool of home educators and often results in deep knowledge of particular subjects).

The news is not all bad: whether by studying GCSEs and A levels at home or enrolling at FE colleges or using OU modules, increasing numbers of home educated young people are accessing higher education. There are more university departments prepared to be flexible than not and the OU offers a way of continuing with 'home education' at degree level. The problem is that in certain quarters myths that equate education with particular school based pedagogy persist. How can a home educator benefit from a degree if she has not been tied to a desk for the previous thirteen years? How do universities assess alternatives, including portfolios or oral knowledge? If the rhetoric of widening access to education and increasing social inclusion is to be more than mere rhetoric then these myths need to be dispelled and universities need to take the time to consider educational achievements that are completely outside the normal system, including oral evidence of learning and portfolios arising from self taught study.

Part three

Special Educational Needs

There are sixty children in this survey belonging to twenty-five parents. The average family in the survey has 2.4 children which makes them considerably larger than either the average family in the UK or even the average home educating family.

Of these children 36 are both of compulsory educational age and are currently home educated. A further 6 were home educated in the past and 3 have not yet reached the age of compulsory education. Of the 36 children who are home educated 30 have been diagnosed with a special educational need. In addition, two girls and one boy have been diagnosed with a special educational need and are not home educated (they belong to families who home educate some of their children whilst the SEN children are in school). This gives a total of 33 school aged SEN children in the survey. Within this group more boys are diagnosed as having a special need than girls; 71% (23) of all the SEN children were boys and only 36% (10) were girls. 40 children in all have SENs (i.e. 33 children of compulsory school age plus 7 who have an SEN but are below or above compulsory school age).

In the total survey there were 28 boys and 15 girls of compulsory school age of whom 25 (89%) of boys and 11 (73%) of girls were home educated. There is, therefore, a significantly lower probability that a girl belonging to a family with a chid with an SEN will be home educated. Some of the 40 children with SENs have multiple problems:

Number of Problems	Number of Children
1	23
2	8
3	7
4	2

The most frequent SEN issues are:

Educational Need:	Frequency
ASD/Aspergers	21
Dyslexia	13
Dyspraxia	8
ADHD/ ADD etc	8
Dysgraphia	2
Sensory integration dysfunction	2
Hearing Impaired	2
Other	10

Chapter five

The Experience of Home Education in Families with Children with Special Educational Needs

Reasons for Home Education.

The home education community in the UK tends to prefer the appellation 'elective home educators', identifying themselves as a distinct group and separating themselves from families where children are receiving home tuition services from their local LEA or where children are permanently excluded from school. However, among those 'elective home educators' who have children with special educational needs (SEN) this appellation may not always be appropriate. Many parents of SEN children do not consider themselves as being elective home educators at all since, unlike many other home educators, they often feel that the problems their children suffered while in school were so acute that they had no option but to home educate and the decision was not a true choice.

In the earlier research (Fortune-Wood, 2005, pp. 28-29) the question was asked of why people choose to home educate of general home educating families. It was found that parents who had home educated for longer gave gave reasons based on the virtues of home educating, rather than the negative reasons based on bad experiences of school by those who had home educated for less than a year. In this survey, however, there is no obvious trailing off of negative school reasons for home education even when families home educate for longer periods. This suggests that the negative impact of school on families with SEN children was sufficiently intense for it to remain uppermost in their minds for years.

Reasons for home education:

Failure to understand the SEN
Failure to meet the SEN
Bullying
Childs stress
School refusal
Failure to listen to parents
Refusal to accept SEN
Philosophical/personal convictions
Parental stress
Deterioration of child's health
Suicide attempts
Inability to get any school offers
Inability of child to integrate or socialise
Unacceptable statement provision
Previous school experience
Personality of child
General preference for HE
Constant exclusions from school
Self-harm

The most frequently stated reasons given were that the schools failed to understand the child's particular special educational needs. This suggests that improvements in training for teaching staff could have a significant effect upon schools' effectiveness. Without a far more detailed analysis it is difficult to know if the second most commonly cited reason, *"a failure to meet a child's special educational needs"* is a result of inadequate training, poor funding or a structural failure to provide properly targeted services.

Inadequacies leading to a failure to either recognise or provide for a child's SEN have major implications for children. One child was repeatedly excluded as a result of behaviour that resulted from his SEN, suggesting that the school was an inappropriate environment for the child, leading to severe problems for the child as well as problems for others he came into contact with. Another child was unable to secure a school place in any of the eight local schools his parents applied to. Parents reported that children suffered stress or, in extreme cases, mental and/or physical deterioration as a result of their experiences at school. Children often felt socially isolated in school, leading to loss of self esteem, and a significant number reported unresolved bullying. The cumulative effect of these problems and combinations of problems led two children in the survey to attempt suicide, one of whom went on to self-harm.

Some parents reported that they were ignored by teaching staff when they attempted to explain the difficulties their children faced, and parents also reported extreme stress in attempting to deal with the range of complex problems associated with their child's schooling. One family reported that the SEN statement that was produced proved to be totally impractical, something that could have been avoided had the parents been more involved in the production of the statement in the first place. One of the more extreme experiences of parents was the following submission:

> *"[the] School and LEA refused to listen to any of the problems I raised and insisted he was fine despite a letter from his GP in support."*

The Implications of Home Educating a Child with Special Needs

Asking how home education had effected the parents and specifically what difficulties parents faced produced the following results:

Impact of the decision to home educate:

Money issues extra costs less income	16
Less stress	8
Given up job not returned to work as planned	7
Less time to myself	7
I do not socialise as much or it's more difficult	6
Better relationships with children & between children	6
Life totally revolves around child; but less personal space	6
Pressure from friends, neighbours or professionals to return child to school	5
Changed my outlook - made me more questioning and politically aware	4
Tired	4
No significant downsides	4
Home a permanent mess	3
New opportunities and experiences for all of us	2
Taking several children to medic appointments	1
Given our lives back	1
Less peer pressure	1
Freed us from school holidays	1

Difficult dealing with child's SEN behaviour	1
Sibling problems re time spent with SEN sibling	1
It has effected my health	1
Got job in education as result	1
More in tune with the way we live	1
Fear of not covering everything.	1

This list clearly shows that there can be many negative effects on the parents. Less income, the loss of social contacts, relinquishing a hard earned career development, or even, as in one case, loosing a business and a home in order to take full responsibility for a SEN child, are all consequences that have ongoing repercussions for a family. The level of material sacrifice and life changing alterations accepted by many parents are remarkable. The internal family rewards for taking this step can, however, be equally great. Improved relationships within the family between the parents and child are marked and what is most noticeable is that despite the sacrifices and the difficulties faced by many families, reduced stress is none the less listed as the second highest effect of home educating.

This, however, is not to say that all families are content about having to make these changes. One family wrote:

> *"I have had to give up my business. We have had to sell our house and move into rented accommodation to free up the equity in the house to cover the drop in income. I feel angry that the LEA is under no obligation to provide any financial assistance towards the education of my children."*

On the other hand some parents have found that home educating their children has led to positive life changing experiences of their own. A number of parents wrote that home educating their children had affected their outlook and political position. Others said that it opened new opportunities for them which they would not otherwise have had and one parent reported that the experience of home educating their child had lead to getting a job in education.

When asked in what way their children benefited from being home educated there were a number of key words and phrases used by respondents. It seems axiomatic that as a child's personality, needs and problems move further away from the statistical norms

Some of these simple categories belie the profound effects they describe. When parents say *"she has made friends"* it is often in the context of a child who has never in her life been able to make close social connections, and whose self esteem has in the past been disturbingly low.

The ability to address a child's special needs in a one-to-one or near one-to-one environment appears to make home education eminently suitable for many children whose needs are highly individual. Personalised education in this context means providing the space to deal with problems as they arise free from the pressures of the social setting of a school classroom. For many children who have an SEN that includes behavioural symptoms this can mean a lessening of those symptoms.

Benefits of home education for SEN children:

less stress/more calm	13	allows "time out" if having a bad day	3
responds well to personalised/autonomous education	10	Time to spend following own interests/thoughts	2
better educational outcomes	8	end to bullying	2
happier	6	More able to follow advice of medical staff like OT	2
higher self esteem/ confidence	6	improved attitude to learning	1
Improved social/empathic skills/more or some friends	6	responds better to non-competitive situations	1
SEN health symptoms reduced	5	More opportunities to learn about real life	1
Life skills improved	4	Improved sleep patterns	1
responds better to quiet learning environments or un-crowded environments	3	less missed time due to illness	1

"They are both calmer and have less 'symptoms' than they had in school. Their education is tailor made for them and the flexibility allows for sudden breaks when they are having rough patches."

"[The] eldest can explore and enjoy his intelligence without time restriction [and is] free to follow his thoughts. Middle child has learned to value himself again, and value his place in the family. [The] family is so much closer."

> *"[He] made real friends for the first time in his life. Discovered and pursued his own interests and made real achievements in his chosen field, has become socially confident and mature and comfortable with a huge range of people and able to mix and play with even large groups of children. We have a brilliant relationship."*

This in turn leads to less stress and ultimately improved educational achievements:

> *"He is confident, happy, and has gone from having Anthony Horowitz read to him to reading Michael Creighton and H.G. Wells for himself."*

One of the most profound observations that parents make about their home educated special needs children is that they are more able to socialise having been home educated. This flies in the face of the expectations of many professionals working in social services departments and LEAs whose most regular objection is that home education gives insufficient socialisation. It poignantly highlights the validity of the response of the home education community that home education offers a more natural, community-based opportunity for socialisation than the artificial environment of school can ever hope to offer.

> *"He gets out in the community and meets real people every day instead of being shut away in school. He can learn about things in a totally real-life context instead of as abstract and irrelevant concepts."*

Some of the children in the survey had extensive medical needs involving either regular trips to medical facilities or complex therapy regimes at home. Others had periods of illness or stress when attending school. For these children the flexibility of home education allows the child's physical needs to set the agenda while still finding time to do an hour of study or to learn informally through supportive conversations and alternative media. Such an education would have been impractical at school, and for these children flexibility is a crucial element to their educational experience.

> *"[As] my son is ill he would miss a lot of conventional school, but with home education we can work any hours we want and any days we want in a familiar environment where "C" is comfortable and trusts the people around him. He benefits as he's learning from a program designed solely for his needs and at his pace which can be adapted at a moments notice to meet his changing needs."*

The sacrifices that may initially be made out of desperation have ultimately led many parents to new, improved family relationships that have flourished once the stress the children experienced in school fades.

Overall families report being poorer, more tired with less time and personal space to do those things they enjoyed, but they also report that the improvements in their children are so profound that they could never consider returning them to school.

> *"I'm skint. I'm knackered. The house is a bombsite, but, I have a great relationship with my kids. It's a huge gift and privilege to be their parent and to be able to see them testing their skills and finding their potential on a daily basis. Seeing them overcome previously seemingly insurmountable difficulties because they want to do something just leaves me awed and humbled. It's made me realise that they are people and we relate to each other in a way that's respectful and cooperative. I've become more political and more politically aware. I've made loads of new friends and this has given me a fantastic social life of my own. I've gotten to do things I never have before like rock-climbing and ice-skating. I've learned absolutely loads too. I've discovered that a hot bubble bath at the end of the day is one of life's most underrated luxuries."*

Continuing with Home Education

It was asked if home educating parents would consider returning their children to the school system in the future. The answers were:

No	18
Yes	4
Flexi	2
Perhaps	2

The 'no' answers were often very emphatically no, two parents wrote:

> *"not over my dead body"*

Another wrote:

> *"No, we have tried in the past, thinking that smaller schools would suit them better but this has proved not to be the case."*

Of those four who said 'yes' two would do so for reasons other than educational

> *"Really need extra income so yes, If there was a school which would give what they benefit from at home then yes."*

And

>*"Ideally for me yes, but for him no, I realise now that HE is the only way he could be educated."*

Even parents who would want to send their children to school make it clear that home education has become the standard by which they measure the quality of other education on offer. This reflects earlier findings (Fortune-Wood, 2005, p.30) that showed that experienced home educators give positive home education reasons for continuing to do so rather than negative school reasons. In this case, parents observing the effect of home education on their children are less likely to return their children to school and regard home education as a 'standard to be met' by alternatives.

For the other two parents who answered 'yes', it was primarily for their children's benefit. One stated that their child was lonely, the other that their child would benefit from the challenge of the routine in school. Of the two who would consider flexi schooling (that is part-time school and part-time home education, one would only consider a Steiner or Montessori type approach, and only then if their child actively wanted to go, and the other was motivated by the need for parental respite:

>*"I would like to send X to school some days just so I get a break. If you have not chosen [to send your child to] school then there is no respite for the over 5's as it is assumed they are at school. You also can't access summer respite schemes except via a school."*

Respite is of particular issue for parents with children with challenging behaviour or physical needs. Only one parent mentioned the possibility of boarding school, but went on to reject the idea.

Relationships and SENs

Section 3 of the SEN questionnaire concentrated on the relationships between parents of home educated SEN children and their extended families. In the first part (3a) we asked what support home educating parents received from their extended family
In answer to this question we had the following replies:

None	14
As and when	7
Limited	3
Not practical	1
Criticism	1

What is most interesting about this question is that the number of 'extended families' who actively criticised the decision to home educate was so low. In earlier research (Fortune-Wood, 2005, p.25) It was found that for the home education community as a whole 31% of all parents' experienced active criticism from relatives. With SEN children this figure has fallen to less than 4%. However, the proportion of those extended families willing to actively contribute might be regarded as disappointingly low at only 27%. A massive 53% were unwilling or unable to assist and another 12% offered only limited support. Just over a quarter of families received extensive support. However, for those seven families who received "as and when" assistance it was very important to them. For example:

> "It makes a big difference. One side of the family are supportive, and assist with the education e.g. craft, gardening, museum trips, or just taking the other kids when we need to just take one of them off for an activity."

One family where the ex-partner took an active role replied:

> "My ex husband comes to visit us in the family home on Saturdays. This is really important as it gives me a chance to share responsibility for a few hours, and gives our son a look at what family life should be."

I also asked what effect the decision to home educate had upon the parents relationship with their extended family. The responses were:

Positive improved relationship	5
No change	9
Negative reaction	5
Difficult at first now come around	3
Made them rethink their approach	1

A third (34%) of respondents said that this made little or no difference to their relationships but nearly as many (30%) said that their relationships improved and one parent reported that it prompted her sister to reconsider the decisions she had made herself. Only one in five parents (19%) said that their relationship deteriorated following their decision to home educate.

Parents are often wary of the reaction they will get to their decision to home educate, and in families with SEN children these relationships can be of particular importance where respite care is an element. This response suggests that the majority of relationships with extended families will not be made worse following the decision to home educate, though a small yet significant proportion of extended families will react badly.

Replies suggest that a significant cause of the difference between these two reactions may not be the decision to home educate but the nature of the SEN itself. Where the SEN is behavioural some extended families do not recognise or accept the diagnosis.

In all cases where parents identified this as an issue (20% of all parents taking part) the child in question was diagnosed with Asperger's' Syndrome. Some went as far as to say that their extended family refused to believe in the diagnosis and instead blamed the parents for being bad parents. Home education was seen as an extension of that 'bad parenting'.

"Certain members don't even believe my son has AS or even that there is such a thing!"

In the English speaking world Asperger's' Syndrome is a relatively recently accepted syndrome. Dr. Asperger himself published his research in German in 1944 but Asperger's' Syndrome did not appear in a diagnostics manual in English until 1994, fifty years later. It seems that a lack of acceptance or awareness of the syndrome among the public causes a breakdown in relationships between parents of children suffering from Asperger's' Syndrome and their extended families.

Support Organisations and Children with SENs

Section 4 looked at support organisations beginning with which organisations people had joined. Respondents said they belonged to the following groups:

Education Otherwise	16	62%	
Local support groups	10	38%	
Unspecified Internet support lists	6 *	15%	
Home Education Special Needs	4 *	15%	
Home Education Advisory Service	3	12%	
Schoolhouse	2	8%	
Muddle Puddle	1 *	4%	n=26
HE UK	1 *	4%	
UK families HE	1 *	4%	
Scope	1	4%	
Hop Skip & Jump	1	4%	

Pace	1	4%
National Autistic society	1	4%
Home Service	1	4%
Islamic Home School Advisory Network	1	4%
Leukodystrophy Foundation	1	4%

* denotes a virtual, online support group.

Membership of *Education Otherwise* is by far the most common (62%) with membership of a local group coming second (38%). Beyond that no other particular group is common though in total 13 respondents (50%) made use of one of the growing number of internet support mailing lists.

It was also asked what they found these groups most useful for.

Functions of Support Organisations for SEN families

Legal rights/dealing with LEAs	12	46%
Finding contacts, social aspects	10	38%
Virtual networks most helpful	9	35%
Curricula, Pedagogy, Resources	6	23% n=26
Starting off	5	19%
Not geared up to disabled children's needs	3	12%
Helping others start out	2	8%

Nearly half of respondents received help with legal issues or help in dealing with LEAs. This remains the most important function of the support groups. The immediacy and availability of virtual networks contributed to their popularity with nearly two in five people specifically identifying such groups are particularly useful.

A small number of stalwarts (8%) stay involved in groups primarily to help others get started. This is supported by Leslie Barson's work on support groups in the home education community which shows that older established members pass on help and support to newcomers who need it.

Respondents were also asked to identify the ways organisations could improve their services to home educators who have children with SENs.

Perceived improvement needs from support groups:

Not sure – service is good	5	28%
Better support for SEN	5	28%
Resource library	2	11%

Improved help when beginning	1	6%	
More for teens	1	6%	n=18
More for gifted children	1	6%	
Better publicity	1	6%	
Dedicated legal resources	1	6%	
Clearer information	1	6%	
No comment	8		

Eight of the respondents did not answer this question which may suggest they were happy with the service they were receiving. Of those who did respond, over a quarter (28%) specifically stated they were either not sure how the support they already received could be improved, or that the support was already good. However, another 28% felt that support to SEN children and their families could be improved upon in some way. Of these 22% of respondents were specifically commenting on local groups. Intolerance and misunderstanding of SEN were at the heart of these comments. Typically:

> "...more understanding towards people with special needs, especially at meetings."

> "They could be welcoming rather than reject the disabled child."

> "Ask more questions to try to understand us."

This was followed this up with specific questions about local groups. We wanted to know if people attended them and if so how useful they found them. Twenty five families replied to this question. Unhappily this important resource was not used at all by 17 (68%) of respondents. Some reported that they used to attend local groups but no longer did so. Several reported problems and even apparent hostility to disabled children.

> "The local group don't want disabled kids to attend."

There is anecdotal evidence that families with SEN children, particularly those with behavioural problems, often face difficulties due to the symptoms which their disabilities manifest. Local groups are run by a network of untrained volunteer parents, sometimes meeting in a home or a local hall of some kind. They are mostly semi structured meetings. They are as important for the opportunities they offer to parents to socialise as they are to the children themselves. Information about local events, legal problems parents have experienced and news are exchanged and important friendship networks are developed, some outlasting the period of compulsory education of the children. This ad hoc arrangement, supported largely by *Education Otherwise* which maintains the most comprehensive support network of local groups, is crucial. However, groups can also be transitory, as typified by voluntary effort and this can lead to local difficulties from time to time. The lack of experience or training opportunities for volunteer leaders of these groups may well lead to problems, especially when faced with difficult or uncommon situations presented by children with special needs, which in turn leads families with special needs children to feel hurt, unheard or even rejected by local groups who may actually be unaware of the problems or how to solve them. Currently local groups have been unable to attract funding for anything other than the occasional event or the purchasing of some small resource item (Fortune-Wood, 2005, p.47). This makes the prospect of professional disability awareness training very unlikely.

Other parents stated that there were problems inherent in group meetings that prevented their child from attending the local group. The stress of noisy group situations for autistic children or accessibility problems were both cited. Three of the 17 who no longer attended local groups found alternative ways of socialising by meeting up with one or two other families on a regular basis.

> "...we do meet up informally with some other home-edders now and again."

While others did not attend the main group meetings, they did participate in educational or social visits occasionally organised by the local group.

> "We go on trips with other home educators, we don't 'attend a group' on a regular basis."

Two reported that their local group had recently collapsed. Due to the volunteer nature of local support groups the cycle of collapse and reformation remains relatively common.

The eight who did attend local groups found them very important for themselves and their children. In particular they saw the group as giving their children the opportunity to attempt activities that would either be impractical or impossible at home, and the opportunity to socialise with other children.

> "[the local group is] great for social contact (even if the boys are reluctant) and introducing activities which they might not have been so keen to try at home."

"I attend four!! One is structured with weekly French, Welsh and drama and other workshops from time to time such as drumming, science and maths. One is purely social and the other two are a mixture. All the groups are involved in trips out, educational visits and social get-togethers – very occasionally just the adults get to go out!! They are an invaluable resource and an important part of our provision."

A growing phenomenon is that local groups are supported by internet communications. Local groups often have their own internet support group so that members can plan events and socialise on the internet. Older children often use services like MSN messenger to chat to friends they have met at their local groups, extending their opportunities to socialise even from home. Some of these child-led self-organised networks are very extensive. It is becoming more likely that home educated teens will swap MSN identities than telephone numbers, and these ad hoc virtual groups are often particularly important to children who might otherwise suffer from some degree of exclusion, whether children in rural areas or those with physical or other disabilities. This phenomenon is one which would bare further research.

A couple of respondents raised the issue of the costs of accessing local groups. Even where group rates for events or activities were negotiated the cost of travel (especially where the child has mobility problems) and entry to certain events prevents some families from participating in everything they would have wanted to.

In terms of whether local groups catered specifically for children's special needs the response was predictably mixed. 16 people responded offering the following assessment:

Ability of local groups to respond to specific needs:

No	4
Variable	2
Yes	9
Difficult to see what they could do	1

Unsurprisingly where the local group already have a significant number of children with special needs the group tends to be more flexible.

"yes - almost half the group also have kids with special needs"

Equally unsurprisingly we people found that some people were more accepting than others.

> *"there were some people who were better at handling them than others."*

And

> *"On the whole yes, though individuals within the group are sometimes not."*

Several people suggested that since home education encouraged families to look at the child as an individual that this readily encouraged integration and acceptance:

> *"Every child is accepted as an individual, so the issue of age-appropriate behaviour isn't a problem."*

However, there were other groups where families of SEN children felt excluded:

> *"Not always as they cannot join in"*

Management structures in local voluntary support groups are invariably informal with many having no management group, constitution or bank account (Fortune-Wood, 2005, p.45). It is, therefore, unsurprising that such groups do not have an anti-discrimination policy. Although a balance must be met with respect to the flexibility that this informality offers and the responsibility the group owes to all of its members. As organisations like *Education Otherwise* continue to grow there is bound to be increasing pressure to address these issues in a more professional way. At present informal structures often mean there is no clear line of responsibility, this can lead to discrimination against disabled children and families (not to mention other forms of discrimination) not as a deliberate act but from ignorance and omission. The question of how to overcome this problem without losing the flexibility that local groups offer will be an ongoing one.

In a minority of cases there is evidence some groups do not discriminate inadvertently, but deliberately. One family went as far as to say that their local group *"did not want disabled children to attend"* and another had such low expectations as to say that their local group *"did not need to cater for disabled children."* Another parent was told that her young child's physical disabilities were frightening other children. In such cases these local groups may be in breach of the Disability Discrimination Act.

Some families would welcome being consulted about how the group works:

"[it] would be better perhaps if I felt able to discuss the matter."

However, highlighting the complexity of the issues involved, some respondents also stated that they found the idea of discussing their child's sometimes intimate needs with others they do not know well, difficult and contrary to their family's ethos of privacy and respect for the child.

I asked those who no longer attended local groups why they had ceased. Sixteen families responded to this question.

Five responded by saying that there was no local group at present in their local area and one stated that the local group was small and cliquey (which may or may not be related to SEN issues). Of the rest two said they did not fit in well with groups of home educators who they felt took militant lines on some issues, and one feared problems of judgemental attitudes having already had to deal with difficulties when their child was in toddler groups.

The remaining six responded with issues of discrimination. The most extreme response was:

"When one member realised X (suffered from quadriplegic cerebral palsy) she was disgusted. The leader of the group refused to deal with the prejudice and made me feel unwelcome so I never went back."

The rest were made to feel either unwelcome or the accommodation was in some way unsuitable or the child did not cope well in the environment.

It would be grossly unfair to say that local home education groups did a poor job of catering for the needs of home educators. Many of those who set up groups have no specialist training or experience of children with special needs, they have no funding to gain training and little time to undertake it even were they to have the funds. They often organise events on their own initiative, taking the financial risks themselves and have to find the cheapest accommodation available in which the group can meet. However, the hurt and exclusion some families of SEN children can be acute and there is obviously a need for local groups to find ways in which they can consider these children when making plans. Given new legislative frameworks groups meeting in public spaces could find that such thinking is incumbent on them and it would be wise for national organisations to assist local groups with developing approaches to SEN children.

I also asked whether families with SEN children found individual home educators supportive. Home educators as individuals seemed to fair better than groups. Twenty-two families responded to this question. Thirteen stated categorically that they found other home educators helpful and supportive. Four said that most people were supportive and two said that some people were supportive in some ways. Three people said that home educators were supportive in the virtual environment of the internet. People were willing to offer advice and moral support but were less supportive in practical ways.

Despite the negative experiences of a few of the respondents 60% were unequivocally positive:

> "they go out of their way to assist you, with true empathy of your situation".

Many families had experienced other home educators who helped families with visits to educational sites. Several families had experience of home educators without SEN children, taking time to explain a child's special needs to their own children, so helping to integrate SEN children into the local group and a number of families developed lasting friendships with people they have met through the home education network.

LEAs and Children with SENs

There is no legislative duty for Local Authorities to offer support to elective home educating families, even to families who have special educational needs. However, neither is there any bar to them offering such support to families living in their area.

Only one of the respondents in the survey received any help of any kind in the form of some workbooks. Two families were unknown by the LEA and two mentioned that they are harassed on a regular basis with one reporting that the LEA attempt to

> "score our son for the curriculum! Also given a list of special schools in the district (still no attempt at understanding our sons actual needs, just going through the motions, ticking boxes)".

In addition one family receives some unofficial help from their child's ex-teacher who loans text books.

All twenty-six families responded to the question of how other professionals responded to the family's decision to home educate. Only 5 (19%) had no problems. The greatest problems seemed to have arisen from medical staff, who displayed significant ignorance of both the law and the practicalities of home education. The medical professions negative response varied between being dismissive to outright hostility.

"The medical profession have been very dismissive and one member tried to force us to put our son back in school."

Sometimes families found medical personnel so hostile that the only option left to them was to change their doctor. In a very few cases families had to change consultants or other specialist staff. In one case this involved paying for private specialists. In a few cases some medical staff, in their ignorance of the law, made threats to the family that they would stop them from home educating or told them that it was illegal to do what they proposed.

Schools proved difficult for three families but on the whole they seemed to understand the decisions being made, even if they were not actively supportive. Only one family in the group had serious difficulties with social services, but five families had difficulties with specialist education services, mostly special needs support staff who were unaware of the legal position of home education. One or two seemed to believe that home education was either illegal or at the discretion of the education authority (which is only the case when a child is registered at a special school).

"At first I was told I couldn't do this, that it was illegal, that I needed permission that I couldn't meet 'X's needs etc. After many months of explaining myself ,providing supportive evidence for our work at home with 'X' and standing up for my parental rights eventually things got easier and now I have a productive relationship with all involved with "X's" care and education."

One family were left with the impression that the reason the education authority did not object to them withdrawing their child from school was out of relief that they no longer had to meet the costs.

"The LEA here are just happy to get any SEN children out of the system so they don't have to pay anything for their education."

Overall, provided that families persisted in seeking to home educate their children, they eventually managed to achieve their goal of taking back the responsibility of parenting their child from the professionals to whom they had delegated it. However, since this survey was conducted among those who were successfully home educating, the difficulties mentioned here raise the question as to how many families are pressurised not to home educate due to hostility, being wrongly told that there are laws preventing them from home educating SEN children or even threatened with social services action.

The next question asked if they and the school managed the deregistration process in line with the legislation. 16 families responded of whom 14 (87%) said that the local authority and the school both managed the process correctly. One local authority was particularly helpful:

> "I can honestly say they were great. Essex LEA are very laid back, are happy for me to send in one yearly update for the family as a whole (I did meet-up with LEA contact in a neutral place once but that was at my suggestion) and have offered to help in any way that they can. They even went as far as to say if we ever have problems with doctors, social services or truancy patrols etc then to refer them to the LEA who will put them right. The LEA also arranges special days for home educated children at places of interest & also special contact days gathering together info, useful contacts & retailers geared towards educational products at one central place."

There were two families who were unhappy with the deregistration process. One was an unspecified problem whilst the other was potentially serious in that the school failed to inform the local authority of the de-registration, which opens the head teacher to prosecution and a personal fine. If a child is left on roll the school continues to receive funding, which is potentially fraudulent. From the home educators perspective a child not attending, but still on roll is a truant so it is essential that deregistration is dealt with correctly.

A further five families said that this question was not applicable, some stating that they had previously sent their child to a private school. It seems probable that the private schools routinely fail to inform the LEA (as they should have in law) that a de-registration from school with the intention to home educate has taken place.

Resources for SEN

Part 6 of this questionnaire was on use of specialist resources. Twenty-five families replied to the first question regarding what resources the family uses. Eight families (32%) said they used nothing special though two said that they adapted regular learning equipment and resources themselves. The most popular single item was software. Of the 12 categories of resources 3 of them were associated with computers: 5 listed websites, 5 listed computer-linked learning aids (magnifying scanners, big key keyboards and screen readers) and 2 listed online support as playing a major role in the education of their children. Only one child had received a significant grant (for a computer and other related equipment) helping towards the costs of a learning disability. Three families made use of speech therapists; one used speaking books and one had a regular consultation with a paediatrician. Three families used specialist books.

Families were then asked what additional resources they felt they needed. Twenty-five families responded to this question and a wide range of resources were identified. Two families (8%) said that they needed nothing and another two said that they were not sure what could help them. The most frequently identified additional resource that families would like access to were various forms of free specialist medical and therapeutic help (physiotherapy, occupational therapy, speech therapy, music therapy and SALT [Speech And Language Therapist]). Although many of these are medical in nature accessing them is often linked to attendance at school. Parents often need to purchase therapeutic specialists and many others would clearly like to but cannot afford to do so. Three parents identified respite care, highlighting the personal cost to parents who are home educating special needs children. The remaining 7 categories were:

Free non LEA assessments	1	Specialist books	2
Voice supported software	1	Child psychiatric assessment	1
Specialist tutors	2	SEN children's centre	1
Advice and guidance	2		

Many parents of SEN children feel aggrieved that having opted out of what was inadequate and sometimes damaging LEA/school provision, other elements of LEA provision that they continued to need were also taken away. Occasionally, some forms of therapeutic medical care are provided within the school setting and when the child is withdrawn that is lost, leaving the parents to find private alternatives out of their own pocket. It could be that this is legally challengeable but some parents are clearly overwhelmed and feel unable to take on the two big monoliths of the Local Education Authority and NHS trust.

The issue of Statements plays a significant role in the lives of many special needs children, so the next question was about statements and whether families want these maintaining or not. Statements of special educational needs were originally intended to force education authorities to provide for the special needs of children registered at state schools. Section 4 of the statement identifies what it is that the local education authority must provide. However, since the educational psychologists who undertake the assessments are employed by the LEA, these statements are effectively offers of what the education authority can afford. Lady Warnock has publicly stated that statements have failed to achieve what was hoped of them.

Additionally, a small minority of LEAs misunderstand the powers of a statement and its relationship to Section 7 of the 1996 Education Act. Some authorities think that because the Education Act states that parents must cause a child to receive an education suitable to the child's special educational needs, then it becomes incumbent on home educating parents to provide what is detailed in section 4 of the Statement. This is not the case. Parents must provide an education that meets the child's needs, but they are not required to do so in the form identified in the statement. This is a particularly important point when the Statement identifies a particular school. Occasionally an education authority will use the Statement to try to prevent a family home educating their child because a school is named as part of the provision of need. Statements force LEAs to act, not parents.

Other education authorities also use Statements as a way of gaining access to the child, forcing the family to allow access to the child to enable follow up reviews of the statement. However, the law is quite clear here. If the Statement is maintained it must be reviewed annually but the LEA has no power to force the family to take part and least of all to present their child for assessment. Under these circumstances reviews becomes a paper exercise and of little practical use. However, for those families who are unaware of their legal rights in this highly complex area Statement reviews can be a tool by which education authorities overstep their powers. In the vast majority of cases such action is *ultra vires* and probably contrary to the families right to a private family life. Since SEN children should be treated in the same way as other home educating families who cannot be forced to accept home visits, such action may also be contrary to the Disabilities Discrimination Act.

Some education authorities go as far as to try to create a statement when the child is withdrawn, even when they have previously denied requests for a statement from the parents while the child was in school.

"Funnily enough we couldn't get one while he was in school. Then when we withdrew to home educate X the LEA suddenly wanted to statement him. They stopped the process when I pointed out that neither the parents nor the school had requested it – so they didn't actually have a valid legal reason for statementing!"

Some parents of statemented children question the usefulness of statements. They seem to have no real purpose either in provision or assessment.

Seven (27%) of the sample did not answer this question. Of the remaining nineteen families, thirteen did not have Statements. Of those remaining six with statements 50% wanted their Statement ending. One (17%) was not bothered either way as they knew that the Statement had no real effect. Two (33%) wanted to continue their child's Statement.

Other Forms of Support for SEN

Finally I asked what other support families of SEN children used. Twenty-two families answered this question of whom several gave general answers. Nine (41%) of families said they had no other support and eight families (36%) highlighted the importance of family and friends. The cooperation of the whole family is clearly crucial to home educating a special needs child as for many parents there appear to be few alternative sources of respite or even moral support. Two families listed email lists (9%) and the remainder listed libraries, local support group, special needs sports group, private SALT and national special needs support groups (though each of these was mentioned by only one family).

Nine families took the opportunity to add a comment at the end of the questionnaire. Several took the opportunity to highlight their reasons for withdrawing children from the state school system.

> *"It is very sad that so many parents in this country feel that the only way to give their children a fair chance in life is to take them out of the discriminating and test score obsessed education system that has invaded our schools. My children are bright, intelligent and articulate, but because they find reading and writing difficult, they were made to feel inferior or that they weren't trying. That is cruel and soul destroying, and it is happening to thousands of children on a daily basis. They say that your school days are the happiest of your life – well, eleven years is a hell of a long time if this happens not to be the case!"*

> *"If there was a hope of adequate provision in schools, I am sure that we would not be home educating now for career and financial reasons. My husband now works very long hours to support us. However, now that we are home educating we have no intention of going near a school ever again. Some of the teachers are great, but the system sucks and do you know what bugs me? We are paying for them!"*

> *"Home education is essential where state schooling is not flexible enough to include your child; the rigidity of the state system excludes children, especially those with special needs."*

Others took the opportunity to highlight the condescending treatment they received from professionals working in the health service and education authorities.

> *"My daughter is highly intelligent but as soon as 'professionals' cotton on to (her 'different-ness') their gaze is excruciating. They assume you no longer know anything about your child and that they hold all the knowledge about X's diagnosis. They look at what you are doing and every decision you make with your child as if it is only them who know the best one to take. You feel like you are in a goldfish bowl. They assume that they can tell you what to do with your child. This is the treatment we have received so far from the NHS at least."*

One parent identified the need for funding.

> *"If school does not suit a child for whatever reason then the funding that the school got for your child should follow the child and be redirected to you for resources."*

Finally, two parents wanted to state how important and how much they enjoyed home educating their children. Despite the fact that many families of SEN children have sometimes extremely negative experiences that force them into the decision, and despite the fact that they continue to face more problems than 'average' home educators, whether within the home education community itself or from education or health professionals. It was obvious that the commitment to these children and the extent to which parents are willing to do whatever is needed to deliver the best education and life experiences to their children was the most persistent theme of this part of the research.

References:

Asperger's Syndrome Diagnosis (March 2006) –
http://www.aspergers-
syndrome.org.uk/modules.php?name=News&file=article&sid

Barson, L. (2004) *Communities of Practice and Home Education Support Groups*, paper delivered to British Education Research Association Annual Conference, University of Manchester, Sept. 2004.

CAMPBELL AND COSANS v. THE UNITED KINGDOM: Sentence 2 of Protocol 2, Article 1 of the European convention of human rights quoted in Paragraph 36 of CAMPBELL AND COSANS v. THE UNITED KINGDOM - 7511/76;7743/76 [1982] ECHR 1 (25 February 1982) www.worldlii.org/eu/cases/ECHR/1982/1.html
See also - Kjeldsen, Busk Madsen and Pedersen judgment (p. 26, par. 53): quoted in CAMPBELL AND COSANS v. THE UNITED KINGDOM - 7511/76;7743/76 [1982] ECHR 1 (25 February 1982) www.worldlii.org/eu/cases/ECHR/1982/1.html

DfES figures (2004) - http://www.dfes.gov.uk/rsgateway/DB/VOL/v000538/ed_train_final.pdf - table 2.2 p. 22 & p.11

EO Newsletter (2003) 'And so to university' in *Education Otherwise* Issue 154 October 2003

Fortune-Wood, M.C., (2005) *The Face of Home-based Education 1: Who, Why and How?*

Fortune-Wood, M.C., (2006) 'Educational Philosophies and their legal significance' in *Home education* Issue 2 May 2006

The Guardian (2004): *Home education needs monitoring*, The Guardian 29th of July 2004

Llewellyn G, (1997) *The Teenage Liberation Handbook*, Element Books, Shaftsbury.

Meighan, R. (1992) *Learning from Home Based Education*, Nottingham: Education Now, p.2

Meighan R, (1997) *Natural Parent Magazine No2*, Dec.

NFER website at www.nfer.ac.uk/about-nfer/

See also: www.nfer.ac.uk/research-areas/pims-data/outlines/home-educated-children.cfm

Nottingham LEA guidance on de-registration: www.nottinghamschools.co.uk/eduweb/schools/schools-template.aspx?id=1150

Parent Centre Website of the Department of Education and Skills: www.parentscentre.gov.uk/educationandlearning/whatchildrenlearn/learnin gathomeoutsideschool/electivehomeeducation/

Southend on Sea LEA guidance to home educating parents: www.southend.gov.uk/resources/EOTASGuidancetoParents.doc

'Teens want to chat' in *Sesame* Spring 2006, issue 229, p.17

Thomas, A. (1999) unpublished paper

Katerina Tomasevski, (1999) The Special Rapporteur Report to the United Nations Commission, April 8, 1999.

Appendix:
DfES Draft Guidelines for Local Authorities on Elective Home Education

Copies of this Appendix are available from Educational Heretics Press on request, to be sent by post or e-mail
Telephone 0115 925 7261
or write to EHP at
113 Arundel Drive, Bramcote, Nottingham, NG9 3FQ